THE ART OF BEING A

BRILLIANT PRIMARY TEACHER

ANDY COPE AND STUART SPENDLOW

Crown House Publishing Limited
www.crownhouse.co.uk

Published by
Crown House Publishing
Crown Buildings, Bancyfelin, Carmarthen, Wales, SA33 5ND, UK
www.crownhouse.co.uk
and
Crown House Publishing Company LLC
6 Trowbridge Drive, Suite 5, Bethel, CT 06801-2858, USA
www.crownhousepublishing.com

British Library of Cataloguing-in-Publication Data
A catalogue entry for this book is available from the British Library.

Print ISBN 978-184590993-2
Mobi ISBN 978-184590995-6
ePub ISBN 978-184590996-3
ePDF ISBN 978-184590997-0

LCCN 2015945974

Printed and bound in the UK by
Gomer Press, Llandysul, Ceredigion

CONTENTS

FOREWORD

In an increasingly complex world of education where assessment is without levels, expectations of attainment are rising and a whole new curriculum is thrown into the mix, life for teachers and indeed the children and young people we are working with is potentially hitting crisis point.

We know that maintaining our moral purpose, ensuring the real needs of the children and adults in our system are being met, is the only way to raise standards. Love, happiness, integrity and authenticity are crucial. They are the foundation for true growth.

The majority of us come into teaching with a love of learning and a love of children. We find delight in joining children on a shared journey of exciting discovery and, through this journey, facilitating the development and growth of unique individuals who can confidently head out into a fast changing world. These unique individuals are then able to use the skills gained to negotiate the complexities of life with enthusiasm, energy and solution focused 'can do' attitudes to gaining personal success. As a result, they can make a positive difference, have fun, infect others positively, persevere and enjoy their own unique journey – all in their own way.

The Art of Being a Brilliant Primary Teacher is a book of hope for teachers and for the education system. It is a book that doesn't just outline ideas that resonate but is crammed full of suggestions that make sense and strategies that work. This is a handbook for primary educators – a real reminder of why we came into this profession in the first place and a breath of fresh air that re-enthuses the soul.

This book is that initial flap of the butterfly's wing: the start of systemic change, a rallying of the troops to ensure emotional well-being is the starting point for all involved, a reminder that we can make a difference *and* enjoy our chosen paths.

Sharon Gray

(Sharon Gray is an award-winning head teacher who has transformed a number of schools from special measures to outstanding. Her philosophy of putting well-being at the heart of the school led to being awarded an OBE in the 2015 Queen's Birthday Honours list and to win Teacher of the Year at the Pride of Britain Awards. Sharon now supports schools and is a keynote speaker and an active member of the SEND London Leadership Strategy team and works directly with them through the Department for Education to secure positive outcomes for children and young people experiencing special educational needs and disabilities.)

Chapter 1

ROUGH AND TUMBLE

We have the most wonderful job in the world. We find people in various stages of sleep. And then we get to tap them on the shoulder and be with them as they wake up to the magnificence of life.

Syd Banks

In a nutshell

In a short, sharp opening we introduce reality, remind you why you're exhausted and explain why we're not going to give you anything to do. We attempt to win you over by explaining who we are and why you should stick with us when, quite clearly, you have a zillion other things you could be doing with your time. We mention goose-liver pâté, the hokey-cokey and cricket, none of which are likely to be your thing, but we're confident you will get the wider points. We hint at one of the universal laws of humanity and, while we can't promise you more sex on a school night, we dare to hint at the mere possibility that this book could be the solution. So, for the moment, we urge you to forget about 'Ofsted outstanding' and concentrate on 'myself outstanding'. Away we go …

Hands up if you're in a state of near-permanent exhaustion. Do you attend too many twilight meetings and have too much marking? And, honestly, although you adore most of the children, are there a few that you don't really like? Do your non-teaching friends think your job is easy? Do they drone on and on about a 3.30 p.m. finish and fourteen weeks' holiday? Or, if they aren't saying it to your face, are you imagining they're saying it behind your back? Do you know how many weeks and days there are until the next half-term? Is your favourite thing to be tucked up in bed at 9 p.m.? *Asleep*. Hands up if you have forgotten the last time you had sex on a school night.

But darling it's a School night

Thought so! Welcome to the world of the primary teacher, inhabited by six or seven week bursts of full-on effort, interspersed with periods of slightly less full-on effort called 'holidays'.

The fact that you're reading this sentence is a fairly good indicator that you're already a primary teacher and you've already clocked that it's physically and emotionally exhausting. In fact, let us rephrase that. If you're doing your job *properly* we'd expect you to be exhausted. You're exhausted because teaching is full-on. And it's full-on because you care. And *brilliant* primary teachers genuinely care, with a passion, because they understand the importance of what they do. Brilliant teachers therefore give their all in the relentless quest to educate and inspire. Sadly, there are a few in our great profession who care slightly less. They do their best to cover the syllabus but it's all a bit mechanical. They're ordinary teachers. Their classrooms experience less magic, less imagination and the tap of inspiration is dripping instead of gushing.

Furthermore, we have more than a sneaking suspicion that it's only the very best teachers who will be reading this book. That's not a sycophantic nod to our readers, it's a genuine likelihood. We believe it's only the very best teachers who are genuinely interested in personal development. Every teacher gets force-fed a smidgeon of personal development, foie gras style, via INSET days. But to do it in your own time, under your own steam? What teacher in their right mind would put 'reading a book about teaching' on their to-do list? They'd have to be one of two things: complete nutters or genuinely interested in being world class.

So, which camp do you fall into because, ideally, we'd like you to have a foot in both. We don't want you to be absolutely barking but being a teeny bit bonkers is an important attribute for a primary teacher (more on that later). And you have to *want* to be brilliant. What we mean by this is that we can't want it for you. When you started teaching you will have been given some sort of job description which you filed away and never looked at again. In fact, it's probably a good thing that you never looked at it because it's a big long list of just about everything. Now, we don't want you throwing this book away in disgust (at least give it till half-way) but the next two very short sentences might seem a little irritating.

We want you to go above your job description. And to go above it with gusto and enthusiasm.

No, no, hang on! Don't get angry. Don't swear, effing and blinding that 'I already do more than I should' or 'I already work umpteen hours an effing day'. We know you do! If we were going to sum this book up, we'd say it's much less about your to-do list. So, while we do want to challenge some of your current customs and practices, and maybe get you to do things a little differently, the emphasis is on what we call your *to-be* list. And we promise, as a primary school teacher, your to-be list is everything. Your to-be list dares you to point the finger back at yourself and ask, who am I being while I'm doing those things on my list? Am I being world class? Am I full of life, joy and unbridled enthusiasm, or am I being ground down by parents' evenings or having to squeeze more performance out of the pupil premium kids?

The refreshing reality is that we're not going to give you any more stuff to do. Phew! You will be delighted to know that we're on your side – we reckon you're already doing more than your fair share. The painful truth is that we're going to challenge who you're *being*. If you let that sink in for a moment you will realise it's a 'yikes' moment. Because this doesn't merely challenge your working hours but your home life too. We think the crazy world of teaching has converted too many of us from 'human beings' into 'human doings', where your burgeoning to-do list has become so overwhelming that you might have forgotten who you are. In a spooky conspiracy of the laws of the universe, when you're being your best self a lot of your to-do list just sorts itself out.

But (whisper this carefully because if you say it out loud it might scare you) being your best self is a lot bigger than your career. It is also the key to living a brilliant life.

We've distilled each chapter down to a few top tips, but we're not going to provide you with endless resources, lesson ideas or even an accompanying CD-ROM to fulfil your digital needs. This book is not even very long (we've designed it to be read in one half-term sitting) and it doesn't beat around the bush in an attempt to make subtle points. And while we're on the subject of what this book isn't about, it's not going to tell you how to be an Ofsted graded 'outstanding' teacher or give you a list of criteria for you to tick off until you reach that immortal state. It's not even going to mention the word 'outstanding' any more because that's a label that can be so easily removed during a single twenty minute observation (actually, we do say it a few more times but hope nobody notices).

If being a brilliant primary teacher was about to-do lists and checking off criteria, we'd have a generation of generic super-teachers who were transforming children into insanely well-rounded individuals capable of giving any established genius a run for their money. We'd need no one else to enter the profession (at least for a few decades) and there would be no need for training in education. A simple A4 chart (which, in true teacher complication style, would be enlarged to A3 for easier use of a highlighter pen) would reveal all the tricks of the trade. Problem solved. Ta daa! Brilliant primary teachers everywhere and no one moaning. Yeah right!

We're guessing you're sick to death of change and that being asked to 'think outside the box' causes you to grind your teeth. So, in a bizarre twist of retro thinking, we're going to challenge you to think 'inside the box' by providing some anecdotes and snippets that we hope will make our points in a slightly different way. And guess what? They're in boxes. We hope these thinking activities might cause some sort of reaction – a chuckle, contemplation or maybe even a groan. Most are very short but here's your first one and it's of the slightly longer variety.

In a nutshell

It was past midnight and the man was on his hands and knees, searching frantically beneath a streetlight. A couple sauntered around the corner. 'What are you looking for?' asked the woman, getting down and helping with the search.

'I've dropped my keys,' said the man.

'Where did you drop them?' asked the woman.

'In the long grass in the dark, about half a mile away,' replied the man, feeling with one hand and pointing with the other.

'Then why are you looking here?' asked the woman.

'Because the light's better,' replied the man.

An adaptation of an ancient Sufi story that highlights the common problem of looking for solutions in easy places but not necessarily the right places

So what is this book actually going to do?

With regards to the story above, we want to point you to the right places. If we had a strapline it might be something like 'stop trying to be perfect and start being remarkable'. *The Art of Being a Brilliant Primary Teacher* will remind you of what a brilliant and capable teacher you already are when you've nailed your to-be list. *Yes, you!* Jab a finger into your chest. We mean you at your best – you are awesome! Miraculous, in fact. Sometimes! And then Lucas kicks off, or a snotty parent gives you some grief, or Chardonnay falls asleep in maths and you're blown off course. This book is going to remind you how to have more and more of those good days. It's grounded in pure realism, often provocative, sometimes reassuring and it's self-challenging in that, when combined with a little bravery and risk taking, it will refresh your teaching until retirement day.

So, here is something refreshing right away: brilliant teaching isn't about meeting standards, nailing observations and marking every single piece of work on the day it's produced. It's about moulding what is already there into something unapologetically brilliant. Grow, challenge and inspire your way to being a brilliant primary teacher – grab this book every now and then as a reference point and push yourself in the right direction. In fact, hurl yourself in that direction because, not only will you love it, but you will be the very best that you can be.

Being a primary teacher is brilliant in its own right (we're sure secondary teachers say the same). It's an opportunity not only to shape a future but to develop, broaden and nurture some awesome personalities. To throw a very blunt analogy at it, it's a little bit like Play-Doh. Primary teachers get the new pot that's fresh and fairly easily moulded. Secondary teachers get the 'pretty much set' version that's not easy to budge from its current state. While we're being frank, let's also consider that primary children are less likely to think you're a complete weirdo when trying out something a little off-the-wall or risky. Maybe even something simple like a lesson that's a bit different. Or a resource that's a bit retro. Primary children are less likely to judge and label you for the rest of your teaching career.

So, next up, why on earth should you listen to us? Well, we'd like you to think of us as an author tag team. Stu is a proper bona fide primary school teacher who describes himself as a part-time optimist, experimentalist (is there such word? He didn't seem to care which, in a rather clever way, kind of makes his point) and occasional risk taker. More good news, Stu has experience and is well-qualified in everything from literacy to the Tudors and papier mâché air raid shelters. He's even had a blast at being a children's author and, with the help of many YouTube videos, has recently learned how to

Team A. S.

Andy →   ← stuart

iron his own shirts. But don't let his years of experience lull you into thinking he's old and crusty, oh no siree. He's young, lithe and fresh as a daisy. And in the old and crusty corner is Andy – a qualified teacher who never went into teaching. Andy now masquerades as a children's author and happiness expert who, in a bizarre twist of quantum physics, now finds himself in schools. But what he lacks in chalkface experience he makes up for in next-door neighbour anecdotes (which will become clear later), and believe us when we tell you that Andy takes the subject of happiness very seriously indeed!

Our aim is to take the best of what we both know and combine it into something that keeps the pages turning. We appreciate you're knackered, and the truth is we're incredibly honoured that you've chosen to read our book at all. Andy read a quote the other day that went something like 'Busy, busy, busy, busy, busy … dead!' and thought it summed up his life. And, we're guessing, yours too. Your time is precious and, rest assured, we don't want you to waste it. So, promise number one, no flannel.

13

Ours is a very relaxed approach. To get lasting benefit from this book there is nothing you have to do except read it. If you 'get it' then you will sense a whirring of something somewhere within, and change will feel like the most natural thing in the world. If you don't get it, there will be no whirring and you will feel slightly irritated by squandering 'yet another tenner on a book that doesn't bloody well work'. If you fall into the latter category, we suggest you don't bother with any more personal development books. They're probably not for you (and, serendipitously, that advice alone is worth a tenner).

Hopefully not another bloody tenner wasted!

Most books are about your state of mind. Change your thinking (generally towards the more positive variety) and a life of universal abundance unfolds before you. And we're kind of hokey-cokey with that concept (i.e. one foot in and one foot out). In its purest quantum psychology sense, the argument is that there is no such thing as reality. The world is neutral until you apply some thinking to it, and then it bounces off in whatever direction of spin you put on it. So, the theory goes, if you apply some positive spin to your thinking your life will bounce off into the lush long grass of positivity.

And that's kind of almost true. Sometimes. The really good news is that we're couched in the real world. We're pretty sure that there is massive benefit in retraining yourself to be more positive. But in cricketing terms, life can sometimes bowl you a googly. In plain simple English, no matter how much spin you apply, sometimes shit just happens and life lands in something that isn't best described as green and lush. A 'special measures' Ofsted report is not imaginary. It's like a steaming lion turd on the top of a child's birthday cake – unpleasant in itself but also an indication of bad things to come. And a bit of positive thinking might help around the edges but it's still a brown and sticky situation. As are your massive pile of marking and preparation, the brand new syllabus, the wet break and your moaning colleague. So we're not about pretending these things don't happen. We're more from the Alfred D. Souza school of thinking. He's the chap who reportedly said: 'For a long time it had seemed to me that life was about to begin – real life. But there was always some obstacle in the way. Something to be got through first, some unfinished business, time still to be served, a debt to be paid. Then life would begin. At last it dawned on me that these obstacles were my life.'

And that's our starting point. Positive thinking is all well and good, but positive *psychology* is where it's at. Because the relatively new science of happiness and well-being doesn't mean you have to pretend to be chipper or that grinning inanely through Ofsted will make it go away. It is the study of who you are being when you are functioning at your best. And, at your best, you will be genuinely chipper and more likely to nail an Ofsted visit – and, spookily, the faint promise of sex on a school night becomes more of a reality.

So our advice is to read this book, let it sink in and then do whatever it is that you think the book might be suggesting you do. Which might, of course, be nothing. It might just reassure you that you're fine and dandy. Bravo! Carry on! But, right at the outset, we reckon it's a lot more fun if you accept that life is full of rough and tumble. And, as a profession, primary teaching is rougher and more tumbly than most. But waiting for a good day isn't really the answer. And counting down to half-term in an accidental wishing-your-life-away torpor is definitely not the greatest life strategy. The rough and tumble also comes with a whole load of positives – life changing moments, belly laughs and days of sheer joy and abundance. So quit waiting to be happy and decide that this is your life, ticking by minute by minute. Learn to appreciate it, warts, Ofsted, head lice infested children, wet playtimes and all.

TOP TIPS

♦ Stop accidentally wishing your life away. The average lifespan is 4,000 weeks so, quite frankly, you haven't got enough to wish away. Change your aim from 'getting through the day' to 'enjoying the day'. Or 'only four weeks to go to half-term' to 'how many people can I inspire in the next four weeks?'

♦ Appreciate that even the most inspired people on the planet have bad days. It's perfectly okay to be exhausted and frustrated, occasionally. But if these are your default emotions, you might need something stronger than this book.

♦ Stop treating change as a six month thing (e.g. 'I'll get this new syllabus embedded and then things will get back to normal' or

'I'll get Ofsted sorted and then everything will calm down'). It won't. You are a teacher. Change comes with the territory. Change is, in fact, what you are attempting to elicit in the children, so accept that change is inevitable (possibly even good) and go with it rather than struggle against it (and, yes, we know this is going to be a very unpopular top tip).

♦ Ask yourself, if there was a version of you sitting on a cloud, watching you go about your tasks today, what advice would the 'cloud you' give the 'earthly you'? How would they say you should walk, talk, think and behave? Take that advice.

Chapter 2

THE CUSTOMER IS ALWAYS RIGHT

A bear walks into a cafe and says, 'I'll have beans on .... toast.' The waiter says, 'Why the big pause?' 'Dunno,' says the bear, 'I've always had them.'

Year 4 literacy joke

In a nutshell

In this chapter, we give away the main message of the book, we learn what we already know and Stu reveals his philosophy of education in a particularly deep moment. And, for good measure, we throw in a story about a monkey and finish with your one sentence purpose. But we start with the first part of a trilogy about Andy's next-door neighbour. Hang in there, it all works out in the end ...

Dave is a nice bloke, with a top job, four bedroom house, a lovely wife and three gorgeous daughters. The man has got everything, even one of those watches that he's looking after for the next generation. And a company Audi. And, no, I don't hate him for it. I am genuinely delighted that Dave is doing so well.

Last year Dave took his wife and girls to Tenerife for their summer holidays and I did the neighbourly thing of looking after his house while he was away – fed his cat, watered his plants and I even went the extra mile and mowed his lawn so it looked shipshape for when he returned. Dave and family arrived back from two glorious weeks, so the following morning I knocked on his door to return his house keys. Dave answered the door: tall, slim, suited and booted, sun-tanned. 'Morning fella,' I beamed. 'Here are your keys.' And, in a pally passing-the-time-of-day way, I said, 'How was Tenerife?'

Dave puffed out his cheeks and his shoulders sagged. 'To be honest, Andy,' he said, 'we wouldn't go back.'

'Oh,' I said, ever so slightly deflated. 'What went wrong?'

Dave looked at me through rejuvenated white eyes set in a deeply bronzed face. 'It was really hot.'

He must have seen my slight shake of the head and double-blink of surprise so he explained further. 'Like, so hot that we didn't see a cloud for two weeks. It was relentless blue sky.'

I wasn't entirely sure how to react so I mumbled the first thing that came into my head. 'Oh! Well I'm sorry you've had such a sunny holiday Dave.' I scratched around for an alternative positive conversation. 'How's the job? You know, that fabulous blue chip company, final salary pension and company car?' I asked, tipping a knowing nod towards the Audi.

And Dave's body language slumped a bit more. 'Have you seen the news?' he asked. 'Redundancies.' He barged on without waiting for me to answer. 'They've announced a thousand job losses.'

I winced. It was hard to do anything else with my own foot in my mouth. 'Holy cow, Dave. I'm so sorry. Have you lost your job?'

Dave wrinkled his nose and averted his eyes. 'It's worse than that,' he said, his voice cracking with emotion.

'Worse?' I repeated, my brain racing, imagining famine, plagues of locusts or possibly death.

'Yes,' he said gravely, with a pregnant pause. 'I've kept mine. Some of the older guys are getting a massive payoff. I'm only 45 and nobody's paying me to leave. I've got to do another twenty years. And I can't face another month, never mind two more decades.'

My body language sagged in sympathy and I heard myself commiserating. 'I'm sorry you've kept your job, mate.' But I had an ace up my sleeve. My final game-winning conversational gambit. It was for emergencies only and this seemed to be the time and place. I called his negative bluff with the classic, 'How are the kids?

Isn't it great in the summer hols when you can spend more family time?' I fist-pumped in my imagination. Take that you harbinger of doom!

But Dave had played this game before. In fact, it's the only game he ever played and there was no way he was going to be tricked into positive conversation. He looked at me knowingly. 'It might be great in your house,' he said, 'because you've only got two kids.' He boasted, 'I've got three. And I bet you've never stopped to consider how difficult that third one is.' He gave me no time to consider, instead charging on, gathering some momentum. 'Everything's on a bigger scale,' he explained, jabbing a sun-kissed digit towards his company car. 'I'll have to trade in the Audi for a people carrier. And I'm working on plans to convert the garage into a fifth bedroom. And the food bill?' he said, arching his eyebrows. 'Tracey goes to Tesco and fills the cupboards and the girls come in and, whoosh, it's like a plague of locusts.'

I congratulated myself on the locusts connection but, truth told, I was reeling. Poor Dave! I noticed the vein on the side of his neck was throbbing with stress as he jabbed his bronzed finger away from the Audi and into my chest as he delivered the killer line: 'Guess how many yoghurts we get through in an average week?'

I gaped, trout style, frantically calculating yoghurt per person per day as he spat out the answer. 'Forty-seven,' he said. 'And that doesn't include the Yakults.'

And that was the end of the conversation. My bottom lip was trembling as Dave got into his Audi and hurried away to his six figure salary job. I mean, that's a helluva lot of yoghurt. And as he sped off I felt a bit sorry for him because, you see, that's how things always work out for Dave.

And then I realised he'd done it again! He'd got me. Or, rather, I'd let Dave get me. He'd captured me in his negative spell. And I re-ran that conversation word for word in my head. How can having a blue sky holiday possibly be bad news? How can keeping your job be bad news? And how can having three of the most adorable daughters on the planet possibly be bad news? But because of the habits he's in and the thinking software that he's running, Dave is managing to create a whole load of angst, snatching defeat from the jaws of victory, every day of his life.

And the problem is that Dave is normal. You know him too. You might have married him (or Davina – there's a female version). You might even be him! Dave is having what I call a 'near life experience', and I'm left wondering, is Dave the problem? Or is the fact that I let him suck all

Negative Spell

the happiness out of me the problem? And with that conundrum left hanging, I'll go for a sit down and hand over to Stu …

So here we go. Moving on from Andy's next-door neighbour to teaching. And I would like to begin by stating that the main secret to being a brilliant primary teacher is simple: *do something because it's the right thing to do and not because it's tradition*. So, there you have it. Book complete. Told you it was going to be short.

Or maybe it's a little less clear cut than that. Do something because it's the right thing to do and not because it's tradition is fine, in theory. But life is very practical. In fact it's the most practical thing we know. So being a brilliant teacher is about making choices and changes because it's the right thing to do. Hold on to tradition if it's the right thing to do, but question why you do it and why you can't do it even better next time. And like many things in life, it's far easier said than done. So many teachers do something once, find success and then allow it to become an act of tradition that could not possibly be changed, abandoned or replaced. If you can genuinely say, 'I've always done this, the learning is immense and the kids love it!' then we reckon you should continue doing it (albeit with an eye on tinkering until whatever 'it' is becomes world class).

Thinking inside the box ↘

Knowledge is learning something every day. Wisdom is letting go of something every day.

Zen proverb

You're primary, right? So if there was a wonderful story about monkeys and bananas that related to this point you'd want to hear it, wouldn't you?

A wonderful story about...

And

We're reliably informed that if you want to catch a monkey, you need to book a flight to somewhere where primates live, taking care to pack a cage, some rope and a banana. Once you've landed and argued your way through customs, grab a taxi and head for the forest. Place the banana in the cage and tie said cage to a tree. Retreat to a safe distance and wait. In no time whatsoever the primates will come a sniffing and one of the hungry monkeys will spy the banana, stick its hand into the cage and grab the prize. Now is your chance. There's no rush but you need to come out of your hiding place and wave to the monkey. The monkey will see you and look worried. Grabbing a banana requires the primate to make a fist and its fist is stopping it withdrawing its hand from the cage. Dilemma or what?

The monkey can see you approaching and it has choices: (a) continue to grip the banana and suffer a lifetime in a zoo or (b) drop the banana and leg it. Now, maybe the prospect of prison food isn't so bad because folklore suggests that the monkey would rather continue to grip the banana and get captured. Our furry friend would prefer to hang on to the prize rather than let go. And in a weird sort of parallel universe, we reckon teachers have heads full of bananas – unhelpful thoughts that we continue to think. For example, accidentally falling into the trap of thinking 'Teaching was better in the old days' or

'You can't teach kids on a snowy day'. Even worse, we have *banana habits* – big bunches of things that we continue to do that don't serve us very well but we continue to do them: checking emails ten times a day, moaning about wet breaks or having twilight meetings on a Monday – just because we've always had meetings on a Monday after school.

Rather like our banana-addicted cousins, we sometimes just need to let go. Cut and run. Being a brilliant primary teacher is certainly about learning new stuff but, equally, it's about letting go of a whole lot of low hanging mouldy fruit. Let go of what's not working and drop the negative self-talk. In short, get out of your own way. Commit, right now, to three things you will *stop* doing. In fact, grab a pencil and scribble them here:

I (insert name ………) do solemnly swear, from this day forward, for richer or poorer, to massively improve my classroom practice by letting go of these bad habits:

1.

2.

3.

Till death us do part.

Grab a pencil

... and make a promise of a lifetime

29

Thinking inside the box↘

Anyone can start something new. It takes real effort to stop something old.

But, of course, dropping bad habits is only half the story (adopting awesome habits being the other half). So what exactly is it that makes a great teacher? Is it mastery of PowerPoint? Or delivery of the syllabus? Or using loads of youthful references in lessons? Or lots of YouTube clips and cartoons?

Who better to ask than our 'customers'? And what if the answer was intuitively simple? Here are some massive clues, quotes from children, used in a speech by Steve Munby, chief executive of CfBT Education Trust at the 2014 Inspiring Leadership Conference:

My teacher believes that all students can do well.

My teacher believes that learning is important.

My teacher seems to like teaching.

My teacher expects me to do well.

My teacher is interested in what the students think.[1]

Now look here, folks. It's not our fault that our customers have stated the bleedin' obvious. I'm suspecting you already knew this. But how many can you tick? I mean cross-my-heart-hope-to-die tick? And even if you believe them all, how many can you stick-a-needle-in-your-eye to every single day?

And herein lies the conundrum of brilliant teaching. The solutions are simple. I mean, there are no ifs and buts about those five points above. But 'simple' doesn't mean 'easy'. Let's cherry-pick a few of the statements from our customers:

♦ *My teacher seems to like teaching.* Well, yes, mostly you do. On a good day. But do you like it all day, every day? And do you demonstrate that in your language and behaviours?

1 Steve Munby, Learning Centred Leadership, keynote speech delivered at the Inspiring Leadership Conference, June 2014. Available at: http://cdn.cfbt.com/~/media/CfBTCorporate/Files/Resources/inspiring-leadership-2014/keynote-Steve-Munby-Inspiring-Leadership-Speech.pdf.

← The customers

- *My teacher believes that all students can do well.* Again, you believe this quite often but, come on, there's this child who is hardly ever at school and when they are they're a pain in the backside. So everybody can do well but not them, right?

- *My teacher is interested in what the students think.* Well, of course, you are. But there are thirty-two of them and you're only human so, 'Yes, yes, Amelia. Why don't you come and tell me about it later,' is fine, isn't it?

We're hoping this might have piqued your thinking and that you see what we mean by simple but not easy.

The rest of the book is about instilling awesome thinking and behaviours, so we reckon the best place to end this chapter is Stu's philosophy of challenge, grow and inspire (CGI). If you recall the previous chapter, you will notice he's already used these words.

This is how my CGI philosophy works. *Challenge* comes from the fact that I want to challenge learners, be challenged myself and challenge anything that the education system throws out that I don't believe will be right for my learners. You know, doing it because it's right. *Grow* is the idea that I want to grow my learners into intrinsically motivated people who enjoy learning and appreciate that learning never stops. They need to embrace many types of learning from independent through to interdependent, even appreciating the role of serendipitous learning. Of course, I'm also a part of this growing process as I learn too. *Inspire* is that dream element – the idea that you can inspire learners (which most of us do, most of the time, it's just that we never really dwell on it or consciously plan to do so) to achieve what they want to achieve. It also encompasses looking for your own inspiration and building (growing) on that. And that's often a challenge.

You get the idea. The words are simple and they interweave, overlap, merge – whatever you want to call it. They carry more meaning, weight and significance than a 10,000 word document on what an inspection team consider to be a brilliant teacher. And they work because they're personal.

Dear God,

Help me to slow down andnotrushpast everythingthatisimportanttodayamen.

Prayer for the modern world

CGI is nicely portrayed in *Drive*, a rather fabulous book by Daniel Pink.[2] In it he challenges you to come up with a sentence that sums up the rest of your life. What do you stand for? What are you all about? What is it that you want to achieve? Just one short sentence. Dan calls that sentence your purpose.

What's yours?

---

2 Daniel H. Pink, *Drive: The Surprising Truth About What Motivates Us* (Edinburgh: Canongate Books, 2010).

TOP TiPS

- Next Lent, when everyone else is giving up chocolate or alcohol, announce that you're giving up moaning. And stick to it! Forty days and nights of no moaning will do you the world of good, and will provide hilarity in your staffroom as your resolution will begin to highlight exactly how much low level moaning actually goes on.

- To aid the first point, focus on what you have got rather than falling into the trap of grumbling about what you haven't got. In short, let go!

- Consider your philosophy carefully and always adapt where necessary. If it underpins everything you do (or, more realistically, most things you do), you will feel a better teacher.

- Remind yourself *again* that you will still have off-days but aim to make them rarer/ less damaging.

- You can't change people (and therefore you can't make them positive and happy); all you can do is influence. Sadly, a small

Oh Sod it, I'm going to give up moaning!

percentage of teachers are there just to earn a salary. Sharing your thoughts, ideas and philosophies with these folks is futile and you will end up being labelled a moron. Pick your work buddies carefully.

♦ I know a ridiculously gifted teacher who left a school. It took the school approximately three years to fully recover from her departure. Aim to be *that* type of teacher.

♦ Remember children spell 'LOVE' as 'TIME' (we told you standards of spelling were slipping!).

Chapter 3

HAPPINESS HABITS

If ignorance is bliss, you must be experiencing near constant orgasm.

Exasperated head teacher to Ofsted inspector

In a nutshell

In this chapter, we delve further into why doing stuff because it's a tradition is oh so wrong, we hear about a lesson observation that proves our point and Einstein doesn't tell us about insanity. But we start with some of Andy's thoughts about your happiness set point not actually being 'set' and challenge you to be the shining light of your staffroom.

Let's indulge in a classic family story witnessed up and down the land. If you've got kids, you'll be familiar with it. If you've not, you'll still be familiar with it. Picture the typical hectic Monday morning scene as the family goes through their 'getting ready for school and work' routine. And then, while mum is simultaneously making packed lunches and ironing shirts, the daughter pushes away her untouched and now silent Rice Krispies and utters the dreaded, 'I'm not feeling very well.' She makes sure to put on her feeble voice as part of the convincer strategy.

Of course, mum is wise to this. It's a game. And her daughter has previous convictions. This mysterious illness often crops up on a Monday when her daughter just happens to have double maths. And there is something else to add into the mix. Mum's day is already full. She has an important and unmoveable meeting so skipping work to look after her 'poorly' daughter is not going to be possible. So mum does what all half-decent mums do – she feigns concern, puts her hand on her daughter's forehead and attempts the classic fob-off: 'You're a teensy bit warm but I think the walk to school will do you good.'

'I'm really poorly, honest mum,' she wails through sad eyes. 'I really don't want to go to school.'

Mum sighs. 'We've been through this before, Angie. You've got to go to school.'

The girl whines some more. 'But whhhhhyyy?' she wails, burying her face in her school bag.

'Because you're the head teacher!'

We're trying to make the point in an entertaining way, but this is actually very serious indeed and something that sits centrally to this book. No matter how much you love your job, and no matter how much you understand that delivering education and providing inspiration to primary school children is *the most important job in the world*, you will still have days when you feel totally and utterly … (we toyed with various words here but decided to stick with the first one we thought of and the one that's running through your mind right now) shit.

There is only ONE pic for it

41

I've been studying what I call 'flourishing' for a very long time. That basically means I've been stalking happy people – following them around, rooting through their bins and steaming open their mail – with the aim of finding the secret elixir of happiness. And get this: nobody (not even the Dalai Lama) is happy all the time. The human being is not designed to live in a permanent state of euphoria and, quite frankly, skipping into the staffroom on a Monday morning with a cheery jazz-handed, 'Don't those weekends drag?!' would be disturbing. So, feeling jaded or grouchy or having a bag on (that's a Derbyshire saying – you can probably colloquialise with 'mard', 'cob', 'monk' and so on for where you live) are all normal and acceptable as part of life's rich wall display. However, if these mildly dreary feelings start to become your normal way of existing, then this chapter is for you. If you leap out of bed every day with a sense of joy and passion, if you sing in the shower, smile at your fellow commuters and moonwalk into your first lesson of the day, feel free to jump straight to Chapter 4.

Still with me? Thought so! And herein lie the two most difficult things for primary teachers to sustain, two ingredients that are absolutely crucial to engaging young people and, arguably, the only things you really need: enthusiasm and energy. I'm going to go a little off-piste and take you onto the mogul run of 'positive psychology' and suggest these two things aren't actually 'things' at all. Plus they're actually about life and your to-be list.

There is something in the science of happiness that boffins call 'habituation' and its close cousin, 'set point'. Starting with the latter, your body's emotional system works in a similar way to its biological system so that when you're hot, you sweat, thus bathing you in your own juices and bringing you back to your normal temperature of 37°C. When you're cold your blood vessels sink a bit deeper into your skin and you shiver, which is your body's way of exercising your muscles and keeping warm, thus raising you back up to 37°C. So, 37°C is your physiological set point. It's pretty much where you have to be.

You don't have to think about any of this stuff, it just happens. And your happiness works in a similar way. Most people have what psychologists call a 'happiness set point' which, in the UK, hovers around the 7 out of 10 mark. This set point acts as a kind of emotional elastic band, dragging you back to feeling mildly happy most of the time. It also explains why lottery winners have a temporary rise in happiness before the effect wears off and they too settle back to the point of 'same happiness but bigger house'.

I know what you're thinking. So what?

Well, I suppose you could be thinking that 7 out of 10 sounds fine. I mean, it's better than 6.5, much better than 5.1 and much much better than 2.0. You could just stick at a UK standard and be done with the whole happiness conundrum. After all, if it's good enough for everybody else …? I'd argue that a happiness level that is in line with everybody else is fine – if you want to be like everybody else or if you live in a Trappist monastery. But if you're reading this book, the chances are you are experiencing hundreds of human interactions every single day. There's likely to be a lot of chatter! You've chosen a profession that is of such importance that you need to rise above whatever the world deems to be 'fine'. And if you have raised your personal happiness and positivity bar to 'world class' then just doing what everybody else is doing isn't going to cut the mustard. Remember the two essentials of earlier – enthusiasm and energy. If you want them in abundance (and I know that you do), you need to rise above mediocre.

But the burning question is *how*, when the morbid obesity of change is sitting squarely on your chest, and you've caught that horrible virus called 'responsibility', and her majesty's inspectorate seem hell-bent on demoralising the very thing they're setting out to inspect, and life has become a punishing shuttle run of approximately seven week sprints?

Getting by

Goodish

WORLD CLASS

Mr Jones never shied away from challenge

Thinking inside the box

Could you be happier even if nothing around you changed?

Well, there are a couple of interesting lines of discussion that arise from the set point theory. This first one is me thinking out loud: what if the set point isn't, in fact, set? What if your happiness level is something that you've become accustomed to and it's not fixed at all? What if it's just 'familiar'? And if that was the case, you could become familiar with something a little higher. Not a zip-a-dee-doo-dah-my-friend-is-in-hospital-and-I-lurve-visiting-hospitals-ohh-the-smell-and-everything 9.6, because that would just scare people. But if everyone else is muddling through on the UK's 7.3 base rate of 'How are you? Not too bad considering', you could surely decide to give it a whirl at say 8.3. And then, still thinking aloud, what if you did that for long enough for it to become familiar, so 8.3 became the new you?

I chose the words in those preceding sentences very carefully. Because 'decide to' is crucial. There are two things that happen when people find out I've got a PhD in happiness. First, they roll about laughing (completely oblivious to the fact that my PhD has therefore made them instantly happy) and then, when they've wiped away the tears, they ask, 'What did you find out?'

And I say, 'Happy people choose to be happy. They actually decide.' And then the hysterical laughter starts again, at which point I've learned to offer a tissue and wait. And eventually they recover and say, still wheezing, 'It's taken you ten years to find out that? Something so … *obvious*?' And I nod. And wait a little. I can see it dawning on them, so I ask, 'When was the last time you got out of bed and made a conscious decision to be happy?'

And the laughter is replaced by a furrowed brow. Their eyebrows sometimes meet in the middle. '*Choose* to be happy? What, like actively make a decision to be happy? Well, I guess … never.'

The classic Bob Monkhouse gag, 'They laughed when I said I was going to be a comedian, but they're not laughing now', almost fits. And it's such a fabulous line that I'm going to use it anyway. You see, the science of happiness is simple but not easy. It's so obvious that we miss it. The choice to be positive is like your eyelashes – with you in every moment, part of you, everywhere you look, yet never seen. And to take you a little deeper into the strangulating undergrowth of the happiness jungle, this choice thing doesn't work the other way. Nobody chooses to be miserable, grumpy or angry. Nobody slumps out of bed with the internal dialogue of, 'I'm determined to have a real stinker today' (I appreciate that it might seem that way but I promise you it isn't). Most people don't make any conscious attitudinal choices at all. That means 'the day' decides how they feel. In which case their feelings are entirely down to the vagaries of circumstances. So, on a good day, when the sun is shining and things are going well, the conditions are right for you to be happy and, guess what, you are! *Yippee!* Until the sun goes in, or you get cut up in the traffic, or you get home to an untidy house, or something else in the big bad horrible external world turns a bit ugly.

Most people are *waiting* for the world to be right first, and when those conditions are met, *then they'll be happy*. But if you're waiting for the perfect happiness conditions, you'll be waiting an awfully long time! The choice to be positive is internal. Without getting overly complicated, 'happiness' isn't real – as in, you can't put your happiness in a wheelbarrow. Neither can you with enthusiasm, excitement or

WAIT watchers →

Miss Kirk decided to do something about her WAIT problem.

confidence, come to think if it. They're internal constructs, emotions, feelings – whatever you want to call them, the truth is that you've created them. They're in your head. And if you've created them, maybe there could be really cool ways of creating them more often. And, if that was the case, you wouldn't have to wait for half-term to be happy. Your 'wait problem' would be a thing of the past. And herein lies your internal and renewable source of enthusiasm and energy. Just sayin'.

Habituation is in the same ballpark. Habituation (or adaptation) basically means that whatever you do in life eventually becomes 'normal', and therefore even the most exhilarating activities, after a while, can become a bit humdrum. Christmas dinner, a pay rise, parachuting, cocaine, Blackpool, a new jumper, your new mini, school sports day, teaching … even life itself. All these things are magnificent at first but then you kind of get used to them. I reckon if you had a turkey dinner every day it would cease to be special. That's why, as a teacher, sex remains so awesome. Because it's so rare!

If you boil all this psychological frankincense down to what I'm actually saying, it means that not only is *choosing to be positive* a rare phenomenon, but that its rarity value is for two principal reasons. First, despite its apparent obviousness, the choice to be positive eludes most people. Common sense? Yup. Common practice? Nope. And second (rather crucially in fact), actively and consciously choosing to be upbeat and positive takes effort. We promised no flannel so here is the truth: most people would really like to be happier and more positive but, quite frankly, they can't really be bothered.

So, I'll round off my little section with a bit more of the bleedin' obvious before Stu takes over with some amazing stuff that is more directly about teaching. *Get bothered!* I hand-on-heartedly cannot think of anything you will do as a primary school teacher that is more important than consciously deciding to go for it and be your best self. To raise your levels of happiness and enthusiasm higher than the bog standard 7.3. Yes, it takes effort. But, my goodness, it's worth every ounce (more later dear reader, but for now I'll tag Stu and go for a breather).

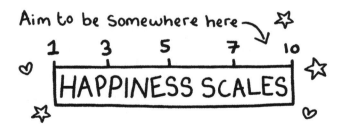

Andy's talking about challenging your own thinking and behaviours so, in a similar vein but anchored in the world of education, here's something to ponder: the merit of the holy grail of learning objectives. I've always been very vocal when it comes to displaying learning objectives in a classroom. Many teachers and education professionals swear by it as exceptional practice that is paramount to children's learning. Learning objectives look lovely and seem to fill teachers with a warm glow and a feeling that they do indeed have a purpose within that classroom. I've often regarded them as a waste of time because I've never seen them have any *additional* impact on learning. Not one single teacher told me what I was learning when I was at school and, you know what, I seem to have done alright.

Picture this: you eagerly await a newly revealed Harry Potter book and, when you get your hands on it, plastered across the front cover is a bright red sticker saying, 'At the end of this story, Harry dies in a tragic broomstick accident'. The story has officially been crushed. Ruined. De-excited. Learning objectives on display simply give the game away. They tell children exactly what they are learning before they do it. Where is the fun in that? They send a message that learning will always be made clear in life and, once you've reached a certain objective, learning is complete. Game over. Learning over.

A cap on learning, if you please. And those higher attaining kids read it and switch off because they reckon they can already do that.

There seems to be this fixed belief that displaying learning objectives will please the senior management team, please Ofsted, please parents and make it clearer what the children are learning. The latter may seem quite feasible until you ask yourself, clearer to whom? And you realise that the answer is probably not the children but one or more of the other three. Unless, of course, you want to argue that learning objectives make it clearer to the pupils what they are learning, particularly when they check back over their books. But, realistically, do primary pupils do this? And does a written learning objective in a book really show learning, or does it just show what the teacher has attempted to do? Unfortunately, visible, oral, written, typed-cut-and-stuck – or whatever else – learning objectives are no guarantee of progress, learning or outcomes. Sometimes they even distort a teacher's view too. For example, Jack has done some brilliant writing and, by magpieing a few words from his reading book, he's really lifted his use of vocabulary. But since we're learning about the use of exclamation marks, this great vocab is deemed irrelevant. Come on, Jack, just get a bloody exclamation mark in there and we can move on to pronouns tomorrow!

Another example. Picture the scene. I was on one of my nosey parker school visits to a classroom and feeling excited about what I could take away and implement myself. It was a literacy lesson and the children were very well-behaved and clearly ready to begin their learning. As she had been on playground duty the teacher was a little flustered because she hadn't had much preparation time, but the class soon forgave her as she wrote the learning objective on the board in that neat 'proper teacher' writing. The lesson continued and the children learned the art of using brackets (or parentheses for anyone who's paid close attention to the national curriculum lately). The children seemed relatively engaged, and then the time came for them to independently show off their bracket use creatively. This is where it started to get interesting for me who, at this point, was sitting next to a 10-year-old girl with embarrassingly neater handwriting than me.

The girl started to write down the learning objective at the top of her page. And with it being quite a long sentence – combined with her perfectionist tendencies – it took her about two minutes. Following this, she checked that her spelling was accurate (fortunately it was) and proceeded to go and locate a ruler. Armed with a ruler, she selected a sufficiently sharp pencil and began to underline the learning objective while maintaining a consistent pencil thickness along the length of the line. Following this, she once again checked that it looked neat and presentable. Success! It was indeed a beautiful display of neatness and accuracy. The whole process took approximately four to five minutes, but you can't rush perfection, can you?

Being fuelled with a mixture of distress and curiosity, I asked the girl why she had spent time writing down the learning objective. The conversation that followed went something like this (abridged – honestly, I wasn't having a go at a 10-year-old):

Girl: Oh, we always do. It's so we know what we're learning.

Me: But did you not know what you were learning when your teacher told you?

Girl: Well … yes.

Me: So is there another reason that you've written it?

Girl: I guess so. Sometimes we look back through our books.

That was the killer. She'd got me. My argument completely lost. Damn! But the interrogation continued.

Me: Ah, I see. Do you regularly look back?

Girl: Not really, no.

Me: But you do sometimes to revise things?

Girl: No. It's just at parents' evenings and things like that.

So there we have it. Four plus minutes of potential learning time, in an education system that seems unforgiving for children who aren't progressing every minute of every lesson, wasted by something so insignificant to the actual learning. The *real* learning. No progress either vertical or horizontal. Would that impress Ofsted? I'm not convinced. And if we get all mathematical about it (or as Andy would put it, on my high horse), we see that this process repeated throughout five lessons per day results in approximately twenty minutes per day. Which is one hour and forty minutes per child in a school week. Or an entire week per child every school year. *An entire week spent copying learning objectives from the board?* The Victorian era ended for a reason.[1]

Of course this would fail to impress Ofsted, or anyone else for that matter. But the point is that teachers and children spend a long time doing

---

1   Let's be honest. The Victorian era ended because of Queen Victoria's death in 1901. But let me have my moment.

something so trivial because it's a tradition that we falsely believe is the 'right thing to do'. It looks good and we've always done it, so why stop?

At the risk of sounding hypocritical, I do believe that there are times when learning objectives are required and it is necessary to share them with students – maybe even write them down in a workbook. If you're learning how to use shade in an art session, a visible objective might act as a reminder to those children with short-term memory loss. And I have no objection, hatred or psychotic tendencies towards those who choose to display them in books because, sometimes, I do that too – although largely because people make me and it gives them a warm glow inside to see it. But what I do have strong feelings towards is the pointless task of children copying them down in every single session. If there was a little more trust towards teachers, maybe this near pointless exercise would disperse into thin air and we could all get on with teaching.

It would seem that this is the point where we need to be introspective. Do we really believe this religious objective-copying nonsense works all of the time? What impact does it have on young primary aged children? Is it just to make the folk at the top happy, or do we really believe that it makes a difference? As Irvine Welsh wrote in the book, *Porno* (I've read some weirdly titled stuff in my time), 'You can't lie to your soul.'[2]

Of course, the objectives aren't enough for us either. We also need success criteria – the only means by which it is possible to achieve the intended learning; the clear-cut path through the field; the spiritual light guiding us through the dark cavern from which we must not stray. I bet quite a few teachers have stopped mid-session and thought, 'Aren't these kids a bit young for all this crap? Don't they just need to get on with learning rather than looking at what I want them to learn and how I reckon, and hope, they're going to get there?'

Then there is the lesson observation. Oh lord. You know only too well the classic situation of the observer asking a child (and Sod's law guarantees it's the one oblivious-to-the-world child) what they are learning, and they respond with what they are doing, which clearly indicates that they don't have the foggiest idea what they're learning, right? The teacher is therefore inadequate, incapable, useless. In reality, a child who responds with, 'I'm writing an awesome story!' is probably learning just as much (if not more) than the child who responds with, 'I'm using a diverse array of punctuation, a range of fronted adverbials and the

2 Irvine Welsh, *Porno* (London: Vintage, 2003), p. 363.

conventions of direct speech in order to be a successful writer.' I know which one would find themselves published in later life!

I'm not a moron. Honest. I'm really not saying that teachers need to do away with learning objectives completely – they're pretty essential to what we do, the core of our educational apple. But they need to be applied as the powerful things that they are and not used as some traditional rhetorical toy. Learning objectives make sure that we, primary teachers, ensure that children learn the foundations they need for life, but without being so prescriptive that we churn out grade A robots. They play an important part in *our* planning – they maintain focus and ensure a broad coverage – so maybe we just need to keep them to ourselves.

Here's the killer: teacher and general maverick Kevin McLaughlin taught a session where he shared no learning objectives and no success criteria. He'd planned it on a Post-it note as the (much better) idea came to him about five minutes before the session started. He did what teachers do best – teach. Ofsted told him it was 'outstanding' practice.[3]

Albert Einstein has been credited (although apparently wrongly) as having said that doing the same thing over and over and expecting different results is insanity. Yet so many of us end up stuck in the rut where we believe that we have a duty to do the same thing over and over. I once heard a teacher dismiss children as 'getting thicker' – nothing at all to do with the fact that his teaching supposedly hadn't altered for the past twenty years! As this book screams time and time again: don't do it because it's tradition, do it because it's right.

And linking back to Andy's point, think about the areas of your teaching that have become habituated. It used to excite you but it has become routine. The stuff that you've got accustomed to and you always do it that way. There might be good reasons for it but we'd challenge you to really question what you do and how you do it. Maybe ask yourself, what would the best teacher in the world do? There will be times when you tell yourself, 'I do this because it's bloody brilliant. It works every time. The

---

3 Damn it. Mentioned that word that I said wasn't going to be mentioned. And the eagle-eyed will have noticed it cropping up earlier in the chapter too. Apologies.

children love it. And there is hardly any marking!' And that's fine, honestly. And the best thing is that the 'best teacher in the world' that I mentioned above, he or she simply ain't in existence. Keep the brilliant bits about what you do, but start looking carefully at those 'Aargh, this again' bits.

Finally, on a wider point, has your school got a set happiness/positivity point? Is there an acceptable level of happiness that pervades the staffroom, and have you settled into that rather than challenging yourself to go higher? As we will see later (and as you will have already realised), the revolution starts with you. You can wait for everyone else to be inspired or you can choose to be the first. Quit waiting because once the revolution's started, others will join!

TOP TIPS

♦ When the 6 a.m. alarm goes, do you rise and shine or rise and whine? Deliberately and consciously *choose* to be positive. Being fit and healthy and being able to get out of bed is the best thing ever.

- Linked to the point above, if you don't believe us, write a list of ten things you really appreciate but take for granted. Health and relationships will surely be on there. And democracy, clean water and food too. Oh, and eyes and ears. Having a great job might feature. And what about the NHS, your car, Wi-Fi and the seasons? Leave your list by your bed and look at it every day. Crikey, you're lucky!

- Lose your wait problem. Change your purpose from 'surviving the week' to 'enjoying the week'.

- Consider your learning objectives carefully. Ensure that there is something measurable (e.g. write), a condition (e.g. independently) and an acceptable standard or quality (e.g. several paragraphs to show cohesion).

- Don't aim to be the world's best teacher; instead aim to be one that the world needs.

- Never forget the power of the primary. You're a role model and, in many cases, a hero. Behave like one.

- Despite it being mentioned earlier in the chapter, don't do cocaine. At least not on a school night.

Chapter 4

MARVELLOUS MONDAYS

Multicultural fact: Despite most people thinking he's either British or American, Mr Sheen is in fact Polish.

In a nutshell

In this chapter, we are introduced to a friend who has turned herself against teaching, we are reminded of the importance of looking after ourselves, we learn a difficult two letter word and we read some statistics. We also go from Grimsby to Manchester, we do the classic *Family Fortunes* survey of 'We've surveyed 100 people, what makes an amazing lesson?' and we find out that Mondays are just Fridays in a different package. But first, Stu throws out a story about expensive watches.

You've probably seen those adverts for crazily expensive watches that Andy's next-door neighbour owns. I say 'crazily expensive' but the price is never mentioned, which leads me to assume that these timepieces cost in the region of a teacher's annual salary. Please note, this section is not written in the green ink of envy, but to make the point let's shift to watches that work underwater. In fact, mine is indeed 'water resistant' and I'm proud to tell you that it still works after it's showered with me. In fact, it also works after it's been surfing with me. It's a pretty cool watch, but I doubt I'm looking after it for the next generation.

Let's sink beneath the surface and explore the world of timekeeping underwater. As I'm no master diver we'll just have to wade along for a moment. (Wade – get it? Ahem.) First things first: the general limit for recreational diving (with some certification and experience) is about eighteen metres. At about thirty metres nitrogen bubbles start to develop in your blood (known among the scientifically inclined as decompression sickness). And, at the time of publication, the Guinness World Record for the deepest scuba-dive was held by Egyptian expert, Ahmed Gabr. He spent four years training (on top of thirteen years' experience) to reach his 332.35 metre record. The general rule is that any deeper than that and you will be dead.

Watchmaker brand Bremont spent years meticulously developing the gorgeous Bremont Supermarine watch, with a re-engineered forty-five millimetre casing to withstand a depth of 2,000 metres. Credit where it's deserved – well done, Bremont! It's a satisfyingly chunky, fine looking beast. Good move. But, under the circumstances, a depth of 500 metres would have been sufficient. As an absolute *maximum*! And I can't help thinking that's a lot of money and time wasted on a surplus 1.5 kilometres.

Look here, folks, it's not just watchmakers. Sometimes we over-engineer situations too.

I have a friend whom I adore. She's great and she means a lot to me. But that's also a problem because I can see the damage that she's doing to herself. You see, Sarah hates her job. On a typical weekend, she will spend most of her time planning, assessing, creating resources, researching, preparing and contemplating. She hates doing all of this but loves the actual 'teaching' element of her job and therefore she persists. And these weekends don't really differ from her weekday evenings, except that they provide a few more hours. Her husband is a supportive chap because he keeps his nose out and lets her get on with it. He would love a bit more attention but appreciates that her career comes first, and he doesn't really want to be hassling such a busy lady. They had some odd vows at the wedding:

Do you promise to let her get on with her marking on a Sunday afternoon – uninterrupted?

And accept she'll be tucked up in her onesie at 8.30 p.m. on school nights?

Will you love and cherish the fact that she's too knackered to ever go out socially and that she'll spend most of her life on some sort of staffroom diet (that's mostly salad except for the never-ending tin of Quality Street)?

Do you accept that the bags under her eyes will lead to mistaken identity as an escapee panda?

And do you accept that stray shards of laminating pouch will pierce your feet as long as you both shall live?

Monday arrives and Sarah goes off to work. She works her backside off throughout the day, encounters one or two things that she hadn't planned for – an outbreak of head lice and an angry parent (hopefully unrelated incidents) – and she finds that the clock faces that she spent hours laminating and cutting out weren't really needed because the class already understood the concept of time. Furthermore, she has to cover someone else's playground duty (typically it's drizzling too), and when she goes to the photocopier the previous incumbent has left it jammed so she spends ten minutes opening and slamming various compartments and getting her fingers into all sorts of inky places. Aarrgghh! Why is it always me?

First, to put it bluntly, it isn't always her. And second, not only is Sarah heavily tuned into the negative side of life but she's knackered, fed up and working at around 15 per cent of her maximum energy levels (if we're being generous). She's even worked out that she will be able to retire approximately seven years after she dies. When Tuesday arrives, luckily she has managed to recuperate 5 per cent of energy from sleeping (after highlighting thirty-two assessment sheets, in various coloured inks, of course) and she arrives at work with 20 per cent energy.

When you do the maths, it reveals some very upsetting news indeed. Within her class of thirty-two, each child is going to get, on average, 0.63 per cent of her energy. And that's assuming that nothing drains any more between the start of the school day and home time. Sarah is probably unaware that the Japanese have a word, *karoshi*, which means 'death by overwork'.

Thinking inside the box

Sir,

I was assisting my 16-year-old daughter with her homework when she received a text from Mum, which read: 'What do you want from life?'

This was an unexpected and profound question for an exam-sitting teenager. We debated various answers – wealth, fulfilment, love, all three.

Five minutes later, she received a second message, blaming predictive text for correcting the word *Lidl*.

Letter in *The Telegraph* (14 May 2015)

Sarah isn't alone. Whenever I tell the story, it's often met with comments like, 'Sounds like me!' or 'Isn't that what we all do?' and it's a heartbreaking thing to hear. Should the workload really be that bad? Is Sarah doing things properly? Is Sarah an awful teacher? No, no and no!

Like many others, Sarah is stuck in an evil whirlwind of tradition, unhappiness and repetition. She's found a routine and lifestyle that just about works – it gets her through the weeks, and half-term gives just enough time to recover from the illness brought on by exhaustion. But here's the rub. Routine is important. Your mind craves order and stability to the point where you subconsciously instil a whole load of habits and repetitive behaviours that are automatic. So, for example, typically your alarm will be set for a certain time and, if you've got a family there will be an order in which you file into the bathroom. If that order is disrupted then your morning goes haywire. And then you sit at the breakfast table (you have a place that's yours and you don't alternate who sits where) and you nom the same breakfast cereal with the same skimmed or semi-skimmed milk, slurping the same tea or coffee, most likely drinking it from your favourite mug. And then you journey to work, getting stuck in the same queues, listening to the same radio station and, if you're lucky, bagsying your usual car parking space. That's your routine of getting out of bed and travelling to work. I could hazard a guess about the pattern of your entire day, ending in what time you like to go to bed and which side of the bed you *always* sleep on.

Rather than challenging you to alter your daily routine with trivia – for example, by brushing your teeth starting on the opposite side to usual – I would like to challenge your routine of thinking. Which brings us back to what I hinted at earlier. If you care to change your thinking, your life becomes a whole lot more thrilling.

Getting excited about life is a good place to start. Quite obviously, the children are never going to feel happy and enthusiastic if you're on autopilot. But sometimes it's hard to get excited when life can be so humdrum. And Sarah's full-on routine is causing her to experience negative emotions. These are like quicksand: the more she struggles to get out of them, the further she's likely to sink. The trick is to accept them and then, monkey-style, let go.

Most of Sarah's extreme workload stems from her own view of what 'needs' doing and the myth she relies on is that she doesn't need to look after herself. She claims not to have time to do things for herself but, realistically, this is because she doesn't *make* time. Unfortunately, she doesn't know the two other big secrets in being a brilliant teacher: learn to say no, and make time to look after yourself (including keeping fit – you have a demanding, high energy job).

BiG secret No. 1:

Just Say: NO!

I'm not going to be naive here and suggest that saying no is easy. I'm very much a 'yes man' myself, as I love helping people out and getting my teeth into new projects. I particularly find saying no difficult because I like to please and get involved with exciting plans. I mean, what reasonable excuses could one possibly have for saying no? Here are a few options to consider:

1 Is there a colleague who you know would do a much better job?

2 Are you working flat out on another project?

3 Are you already struggling to spend time with your family?

4 Would you rather collaborate to share the workload?

5 Would you prefer to postpone until other projects are completed?

6 Would you rather do less and do it well, than do more and do it worse?

If you can answer yes to any of the above, you've got a perfectly valid and undisputable reason for saying no.

People are often fascinated when I tell them about all of the things that I manage to do on top of being a full time teacher, husband and father. But the idea of looking after myself goes back to some thinking from a long train journey where, in a bid to retune out of negativity and into positivity, I considered how I could be most brilliant in the classroom.

It started with a 4 a.m. alarm and a 5.26 a.m. train. I expected to collect my tickets from the self-service machine in order to save a thirty-two mile round trip to collect them (everywhere is a long way in Lincolnshire, except Holland) or some extortionate costs to post them. However, in a moment of sheer wisdom, Grimsby station had decided to put the self-service machine inside the main building, which required a human to 'man' the building and therefore would not be open until 7 a.m. And that really,

really defeats the purpose of self-bloody-service. Oh, and my iPod battery had died and there was going to be no Wi-Fi on the train for my iPad.

Stuart's tickets to serious thinking

After waking up the night porter and grovelling with her, I collected my tickets and boarded the train. Time for some serious thinking, and that started with what night it was. It was Burns Night, and I was going to be missing the festivities. You see, I was heading to Manchester for a course and it would be a long old day. It was my choice to be on the course and my choice to skip Burns Night. I'd made a conscious choice around that touchy area of a work–life balance and I was content with it. Here's what I got to thinking …

How often have you said or heard something along the lines of, 'Children need first-hand experiences to ensure quality learning and to broaden their minds'? Quite a lot I imagine. My big concern is that people usually start that with the word 'children' or 'pupils' and not 'humans'. Everyone needs a contrast to their work, and allowing time to do so doesn't make you any less career dedicated. In fact, it actually puts you in better stead to be the best that you can be.

In the past few years I've directed a show, produced a few shows, presented on local radio, played in a band, performed, written several songs, published articles in the media, written a children's book and invented a solar powered helicopter. Okay, so I might have made that last one up – that's a work in progress. But you get the idea that I've done quite a lot for someone in such a 'demanding career'. And that's normally the excuse – oh, the chains of demand that hold us down!

The most frequently asked question is, 'How do you manage it all?' The truth of the matter is that if I didn't do things like this I'd go insane. I love my job, I really do. But as human beings we need variety. Scope. Colour. We need sides to our life that aren't always work focused. And, most importantly, we need to *make* – not *find* – time for it. Making time is such an easy thing to do, but we often kid ourselves that we can't possibly do it. How do we make time? We're far too busy to do that, right? So we don't try.

What I thought was just an issue for newly qualified teachers (NQTs), but have since learned that it applies to a lot of experienced teachers too, is feeling comfortable about not spending every hour working, preparing, assessing, resourcing, planning and so on to be a brilliant teacher. Your brain needs a variety of stimuli and your pupils want to see personality, so share your experiences and hobbies with them and utilise them as part of your practice. Use your damn talents! It's okay. Unfortunately, Sarah hasn't learned that yet – but it's never too late!

Whether you see it as a work–life balance or a work–life spectrum, you do need to take control and find a balance that works. Olde worlde time management courses (Andy tells me) used to be about being super-efficient: make a list of what is urgent and important and prioritise accordingly. But the world has moved to a point where everything seems to be urgent and important. My gut feeling is that most teachers have reached a tipping point where you can't work any harder, and you know that a government claiming to 'reduce' workload will unintentionally end up doing the exact opposite.

Our argument is not that you don't have to be efficient – of course you do, it's a prerequisite to brilliant teaching. But what happens when you devise a super-duper efficient system to sort your emails? You're not rewarded with time off, you are just cursed with even more emails and a never-ending deluge of stuff. You know what you're capable of and how much you can take on. Try taking on a hobby that is flexible, as you never know what's around the corner, but make sure that you find something you genuinely enjoy. If going to the gym is more of a chore than a gripping moment in your life – don't go. If learning to play the violin is something quick that you can do half-heartedly once a week – don't do it. Be honest with yourself, make yourself happy and utilise it in your practice because only then will you be the brilliant teacher that you can be.

Thinking inside the box

Maybe self-improvement is a waste of time. Maybe self-remembering is where it's at.

With the clinically depressed and the overworking Sarahs placed to one side, every teacher strives to deliver the very best lessons that they can. And while they have an idea of what a lesson looks like from their planning, it's only during the delivery that they truly know what category this lessons falls into. I guess that is the excitement of teaching – every lesson is like results day for the hard work that has gone into it. Amazing results come through careful planning, but we reckon there is also a hefty element of luck that:

- The children respond behaviourally as intended.

- Most, if not all, of the children learn and make progress.

- The resources work as intended.

- There are no negative unplanned events.

- Timings are precise enough to allow success.

- The teacher has enough energy to make it work regardless.

In other words, there is a very small chance of delivering an incredible lesson and an even smaller chance of delivering them consistently. In reality, teaching one single incredible lesson is a bloody great risk to anyone's sanity. Don't forget, though, that the list above stems from the opinion of a primary school teacher and a happiness boffin. So, we decided to put on a brave face, prepare ourselves both mentally and physically and face our harshest critics. Ofsted? No. A group that can be even more fierce than her majesty's special ones – the pupils (or, as Andy rather annoyingly likes to call them, our 'customers').

We agreed that we would start asking children about the lessons, learning and journey that they were experiencing. And not just phatic questions that encourage a fickle response ('Did you enjoy that lesson?') but questions and discussions that would truthfully reveal what made the most brilliant of teaching. While some questions were more geared towards older pupils, the majority could be applied to any age.

♦ What made learning difficult in that session?

♦ How useful was I? Could I have left the room for a while?

♦ If you were teaching that session, what would you have done for everyone in the room?

♦ Was I a good role model, or did I just tell you what to do?

♦ Is there anything that you can now do that you couldn't before?

The questions were carefully worded in a bid to elicit the most realistic answers. They were almost worded 'negatively' in order to try to draw truth – for example, 'Is there anything that you can now do?', rather than 'What can you now do?', didn't ask for something that may not have truthfully been there.

Of course, not every child had 'progress' in the forefront of their mind when answering. And we know that it is vital – we're told far too frequently. But when we remind ourselves that athletes don't make progress during *every* training session or that, sometimes, we need to go back to strengthen foundations before commencing further building work, we realise that children don't need to answer with progress in mind. You could even argue that, mostly, progress comes with enjoyment, happiness and self-esteem.

The responses were varied yet all highly relevant. We discovered that some stuff we had assumed to be 'fun' for primary aged children was, in fact, quite naff. On the other hand, we found out that some activities we had done completely off the cuff went down a treat. So, while our meticulous planning didn't always work as intended, we gained a much more accurate insight as to where our planning efforts needed to go in the future. And the funniest thing of all: the job suddenly became much, much easier.

I hardly dare to call this small sample of unfunded and unrepresentative investigation 'research'. It was carried out in two classrooms in the same county. It was performed sporadically, randomly and in the most uncontrolled of unscientific environments. But what matters is that this was shockingly realistic and personal. It was tested on what was directly affected by us (our classes) and the results were used to alter what we directly affected (our classes). You get the point, I'm sure. Of course, I'm not advocating no-notice pupil-led inspections. I'm not even suggesting that we encourage everyone to empower pupils to make formal judgements on us. All I'm promoting here is that you form a realistic idea of what you are like in the eyes of a young learner.

I'm sure most teachers have encountered the situation during a lesson observation where something has gone horribly wrong. Not because it was unplanned, as such, because even the most inexperienced teacher knows that teaching is full of unplanned surprises on a daily basis. I'm referring to one of those situations that just happens to catch you out, or you do something that is a bit trivial and not really representative of your 'normal' practice, and someone judges you for it. Typical. And your usual response is something like:

'I don't normally do that. I don't know why I did it.'

'They normally love doing stuff like this.'

'The kids *always* get it – I don't know what went wrong today.'

'He's usually so good at maths!'

'I wasn't myself because you were observing.'

'I was put off by your array of highlighters on that massive inspection grid.'

But where is your proof that you are actually fairly decent normally? Wouldn't it be good to throw some pupil comments and judgements back at them?

In our small, flawed and unrepresentative study, we didn't have strangers coming in to analyse what we did well and what we didn't do well. We didn't have 'experts' who had spent years reading up on children's learning styles, theories and hierarchies scrutinising our ways with a barrage of criticisms. We very simply asked the people who put up with us on a daily basis how we could make those daily basis-es a bit better.

And, my goodness, it worked. If you want to be a brilliant teacher, be brave and invest a little time having your brilliance properly assessed.

There is, of course, the 'fur coat and no knickers lesson', which is Ian Gilbert's rather fabulous way of describing the lesson that is all-singing and all-dancing on paper but somehow falls several shades below *Chicago* in the four walls of the classroom. So, if your lesson had proper Bridget Jones knickers – you know, truly memorable and with real substance – how would you know? Well, first, you just would. If you've got an ounce of emotional intelligence you will know it went well from the buzz in the room or the chipper attitudes of your 'customers'. But both of us agree that, ultimately, the sign of a good lesson is that the child goes home and talks enthusiastically about it. The learning hasn't finished. In fact, it's only just started because the sign of a *brilliant* lesson is that evening your customer chooses to forego their favourite teatime quiz show, sits down at their tablet and Googles it – in their own time and of their own volition. Or, if they're tiny, they're acting it out at home. The real tragedy is that her majesty's specially trained inspection ninjas aren't measuring that part of the learning. Nobody knows, except the child.

Has your lesson got these?

So, here's something to occupy your dreams tonight: if you delivered *that* lesson (the one the children couldn't wait to get home and gush about) what would it look, sound and feel like?

TOP TIPS

- The moment you start disliking your job (for a decent length of time), do something about it. Don't start to accept it as normal.

- If you know a 'Sarah', buy her this book.

- Practise saying no in front of a mirror to avoid conveying a sense of hostility.

- Don't be afraid to ask pupils, colleagues and friends, 'What makes a good lesson?' But never ask parents. Ever.

- Stop over-engineering your lessons. When you stop over-engineering your lessons you will have created some time for a life outside of teaching. The universe will enrich you and make you a better teacher.

- Appreciate that you are in a high energy job and look after yourself. Eat healthily and take exercise.

BiG secret No.2:

Look after yourself

Try: eating   Sleeping   drinking   moving   grinning

- Appreciate that 'outstanding' requires a big dollop of luck. But in another perverse twist of the universe, the happier you are, the luckier you get.

- Ignore the depth limit when buying a watch.

Chapter 5

THE GOOGLE FACTOR

Ben rummaged in his jacket pocket and pulled out the phone. 'Err, hello?' he said, aware that he didn't own a phone.

Key Stage 2 story starter

In a nutshell

In this chapter, we learn the importance of painting half a shed, we are reminded to prioritise even though it's tough and we glean a very important message from photographers. We throw in something a bit radical from Google and we remind ourselves that trying new things is invigorating for both learners and teachers. We also look at factory farming and, for the oldies, we reminisce about Bob Dylan. But first – Stuart's shed!

My wife decided to paint the shed one day. She's fairly radical like that. So, off I go to work while she starts painting. On my return home, crikey, she's done it and it looks great. Sure enough, there's paint all over her face, an old duvet cover mashed into the grass (because we'd hate for the grass to be painted) and a paint tin covered in dead flies, but the shed looks like a winner. Another successful day in our household.

looking like a winning shed

It was only later that she revealed she'd only painted the sides of the shed that faced the house – the back and the left hand side (next to a fence) were completely untouched. And, to the horror of many, she had no intention of painting them. You see, the rest of the shed didn't need painting to have the impact that she wanted. It looked fine, it did the job and we were rather chuffed with it. Our shed was summer-ready. She had prioritised in her busy schedule and would do the rest if and when she had the chance. Or, more probably, when I had the chance. No one was missing out and no one was unhappy with our half-new shed.

So how is that going to help make a brilliant teacher?

As teachers, we so often lose focus on prioritising what really matters. And the bizarre and often frustrating thing about teaching is that these priorities often vary on a weekly, sometimes daily and frequently minute-by-minute basis. The mistake made by so many is to do what mattered last week (because it's still not been done), rush it so it's passable and then dwell on it, complaining about how busy you are and how drained you feel. That ain't good. Here's the trick: play on the advantage of ever changing priorities. Do what matters at the time, do it successfully and then move forwards.

It may seem controversial to raise this next point, but when you think about it carefully it makes a hell of a lot of sense. Your class have done some maths work on perimeter. Edgy stuff, eh? As you've gone around the class, you've identified which pupils have nailed it, those who still need some further practice before it's embedded and those who haven't got the foggiest idea and are as far away as possible from the immortal state of 'mastery'. Two days later and you've addressed it. An intervention group has been identified and every pupil is making the necessary progress.

The problem is that you never formally marked the work in the books. And because what may ensue from an unmarked page doesn't even bear scrutiny, you sit down to mark them. Before you know it, that's a good forty-five minutes (if you're lucky!) gone into something that no longer matters. Now, if you're thinking that I'm advocating not marking, then you need to reread. The perimeter situation had been followed up appropriately. The impact was there. It's just that the 'expected formality' had not been completed. It seems obvious, but us teachers often fall victim to 'doing the formalities'. But Ofsted want to see every single piece of work marked in an array of colours, right? No. They have even published a response to this myth.

A friend, Jane, told me about the time she almost left teaching because she lost focus on the bigger picture. There was a boy in Jane's Year 2 class who had been having a miserable time and was, apparently, really playing on it. Although he was very much in a minority (the others were quite the contrast), mum was in on a daily basis and, after weeks of discussions and meetings, she started to change her practice completely to suit the boy. Or his mother. That one's debatable.

She started to pull to pieces what she'd done in the past in a bid to try to understand what had led to the boy's disengagement. She started to become overwhelmed with all sorts of self-doubt, anxiety and worry. She'd plan lessons solely around said boy's interests and hobbies, and she'd enter the classroom each morning filled with a combination of hope, upset and dread. While she put energy into engaging one boy out of twenty-seven pupils, she slowly lost the spark that kept the other twenty-six so engaged and in love with learning.

Thinking inside the box

Happiness expert Gretchen Rubin suggests any family is only ever as happy as their least happy child. What if the same principle applies in the classroom?

Another example stems from a friend who never focused on the present. He'd spend ages dwelling on the past and ages considering how he could improve in the future and, therefore, he forgot to consider the here and now. Everything was either regret or ambition and, as such, nothing ever seemed to be relevant. I think we're often guilty of this as primary teachers. Maybe because we're too busy. Maybe because we try to do too much. Or maybe because our profession doesn't truthfully allow time to celebrate what we're good at. But I digress. The point I'm attempting to make is that the friend in question always felt stressed, overworked and trapped. The reason for this was, arguably, self-inflicted because of the way he viewed things.

So, what's the solution to these great life puzzles?

First, and this might sound a bit radical, the truth is that you will never get *everything* done. That's not the game any more. If you let go of this particular habit of thought, it leaves you the freedom to select the *right* things to do. Your burgeoning workload means you have to develop a ruthless streak that protects your time and attention, focusing only on the things that add the greatest impact, even at the expense of other things that are well worth doing. Painting half a shed is a pretty good example.

94

Photography is also a nice analogy. A photographer always knows where and how to focus. Focus is so important that the majority of cameras have an autofocus function. This finds the most logical, largest or most significant subject, or part of the subject, to fix on. If you're photographing a cathedral, it won't autofocus on a daffodil growing in a flowerbed below. What teachers need to do is use a little autofocus now and again to see what *really* matters. As Jane's experience shows us, it's a dangerous spiral if we don't.

Time is certainly an issue. If you add up classroom time, after-school activities, meetings, marking, prep and all the other baggage that comes with the territory, many teachers work fifty hours a week or more. So, if time is limited, focus becomes crucial. And I know it goes against your work ethic, but deciding *not* to do things is more important than ever.

Interestingly, Jane eventually sussed this one out and, as the academic year ended, she was flooded with cards and gifts from children and parents explaining what a phenomenal year they'd had and how their children had blossomed into fantastic, intrinsically motivated learners who loved school. Nice one, Jane! And she'd nearly given it all up. And the other unnamed guy? He never attempted to focus and left teaching to pursue photography.

Irony's great. Whatever you do, try to focus on what really matters, but never forget how rapidly that changes.

Perseverance pays off!

Thanks

But, I hear you scream, 'How can I focus when there are so many things to focus on?' It's worth reminding ourselves once again that this book is not about telling anyone what to do. It's all about developing a mindset to try new things with a view to making education the most powerful entity that it can be. With that in mind, I have this thing about what I call 'factory farmed education'. Classrooms piled high with learners, crammed in, force-fed a syllabus that, to be fair, can be a little bland. But we make it as efficient and painless as possible with the aim of mass producing adults who are capable of holding down a job and paying taxes so they can contribute to the upkeep of the factory farming system.

I'm not ranting about the system as such. Not really. It did sort of work, back in the day, which is probably why UK policy often seems to look backwards when it comes to education. Ah yes, the Victorian times. The empire. That's when Britain was great, so let's just do that again. But the factories have closed and kids aren't allowed up chimneys any more.[1] The world is more nimble, business is more footloose and Mr Dylan was right about the times – they sure are a changin'. In the business world, there is less need to follow orders and more need to do exactly the opposite: think for yourself.

Children starting primary school today will be retiring at the end of the century. I don't know about you, but I can't imagine what the world will be like in five years' time, never mind in 2100. I know the syllabus is important and that people need to know stuff. But in a world where information is at your fingertips, I can't help thinking that school needs to be about instilling a desire to learn, slotting bits of learning together to find solutions and about a whole load of important personal characteristics such as adaptability, resilience, positivity, optimism,

---

1 I've asked Stu to see if that holds for Lincolnshire.

creativity and suchlike. And therefore a more 'free range' approach to education might be more appropriate.

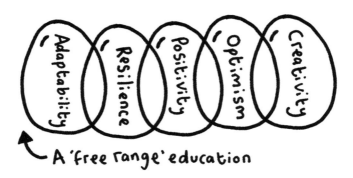

A 'free range' education

I know the national curriculum can be a swine at times, with its Roman numerals demands and Pudding Lane pub quiz facts it wants children to know, but in fact it actually offers a lot of freedom and it can be as creative as you let it be. With that in mind, it's worth looking at an approach I took a few years back because I wanted to empower learners to learn about the things that intrigued them as individuals. I wanted to win over every single pupil by providing them with an opportunity to learn in the context of the stuff they loved. It focused around both independence and interdependence. To some teachers, independence is giving out a worksheet and a child completing it on their own. Interdependence is giving out a worksheet and a child working through it with a partner for the 'hard bits'. Hopefully, those sorts of teachers aren't reading this book. Then again, maybe they should.

Although there are hundreds of complex and highly academic definitions, independent learning is simply about learners learning stuff (not just facts) through their own efforts, while developing skills to be critical and skills to investigate further. On the other hand, interdependent learning is basically learning stuff that can't be learned without the input, experience or support of others. It's fairly uncontroversial to say that the majority of teachers know how effective these types of learning can be, so most of us naturally flip between independent and interdependent learning in our day-to-day work. Getting one of them to be properly successful is tough enough though, so what about combining them both? As a big advocate of creativity, I read about Google's concept of '20 per cent time'. In short, Google offered its engineers 20 per cent of their timetable to work on their own projects – things they were truly passionate about and not necessarily in their job description. Brave move. And I couldn't help thinking, if a company as massive as Google can get this working successfully, it's got to work for education too. And it fitted my challenge, grow and inspire philosophy very well indeed.

It came as a great shock to discover that some teachers out there were already using CGI. They hadn't necessarily given it an official title but they were trying to sail with it. So, my revolutionary idea wasn't technically my revolutionary idea at all. The point though is that I was going to *make* this my revolutionary idea by tweaking, mastering, analysing and prodding. I planned to launch 20 per cent time in my classroom at the start of the fifth term and, naturally, I wanted to make a big thing of it to the children. If I was going to spend days crafting this, I wanted them to sodding well fall in love with it! After announcing the inclusion of it into the timetable (one or two hours per week on an already highly flexible timetable), the children were buzzing with ideas and interests. They were discussing potential projects with their parents, gathering resources or researching relevant material. Of course, I had to ensure that a few guidelines were in place to maintain standards, and they were:

- It must be some type of learning and you must document it in your homework diary.

- This work, and all other work, must be of the highest standard.

- It may be continued at home.

- You have access to most resources as long as the use can be justified.

♦ You may work in groups of up to four
  people.

Once I felt prepared and confident with the launch, I presented the idea to my head teacher – preferring to show that I was organised, ready and bursting with enthusiasm, rather than just discussing a half-considered idea. Luckily, I was supported and an agreement was reached that, should it prove unsuccessful, I would drop it immediately. This would be a tragic dent in my pride, but nevertheless it was something I was willing to put on the line to make a difference.

Each child had a three minute 'meeting' with me to discuss and document their ideas and, most importantly, what they hoped to learn and achieve through their project. They had to be critical too – what did they need to improve on? How would they ensure that they were learning and challenging themselves? Each child left the meeting with a clear idea of their learning and a rough idea of what the success criteria would look like. The best part? Each and every child had an intrinsic desire to learn. Promise.

As the 20 per cent time sessions began flowing over the next couple of weeks, the atmosphere was remarkable and very genuine. I spent a good twenty minutes just sitting and observing the children – so powerful but something we just don't seem to make time for once they leave foundation stage. Did the children even need me any more? I went to the staffroom, put my feet up and booked a holiday. Yes, I am joking. In reality, these were the busiest sessions I've been involved in. I'd go home overwhelmed with knackeredness. Trying to effectively monitor so many different projects to ensure definite, powerful learning wasn't a laidback task. But it was lovely: I enjoyed myself (as did the children) and therefore I had no qualms about putting energy into it. Advice and feedback came naturally too but from other children rather than me. This was peer assessment on a whole new and highly realistic level (which, admittedly, was something I'd previously tried to get right for months).

Projects began to take shape as the weeks went by and the children rarely lost focus. If they did, they soon got it back by looking at what they had set out to learn and improve on. Then we set new objectives for greater progress. A proportion of the learning that took place was also serendipitous (90 per cent of my own learning happens through this learning style!) – learning things they hadn't necessarily set out to learn in the first place. The range of interests in my class included films, cars, animals, console games, sewing, cookery and so much more. Children ended up producing books, magazines, websites, guides, film reviews, storybooks, artwork and presentations. The second greatest thing was that the content was of an exceptionally high quality. The first greatest thing was 9-year-old children caring about and managing their learning in such a mature way.

Any new initiative or something a little different is never without its sceptics – those people who challenge an idea and question the need for change (sound familiar?). But I've started to realise that, without them, concepts such as this would lack strength. People certainly questioned why I wanted to implement this initiative. Answering that was easy. Unfortunately, extrinsic motivation can only go so far in education and, above all else, I want my pupils to be people who enjoy learning. In fact, don't we all?

Attitudes within the class improved too. Children worked hard on their other work to ensure 20 per cent time happened, and their standards were higher. If their own projects were so good, they must be capable of doing that with other work too, right? And the concept also catered for children with special educational needs or those who struggled with staying on-task. With a little careful monitoring from me they just got on, seeking support as and when it was required from whoever they felt was right for the job. In fact, they really shone.

Through 20 per cent time, a class of intrinsically motivated learners developed who strived to make themselves proud without any fear whatsoever of making mistakes. They were flexible, found solutions to problems and they offered realistic advice to their peers – appreciating the importance of interdependence within society. Their projects were memorable and they were unique and bursting with creativity.

Needless to say, 20 per cent time won't work with every single class, in every single school, in every single year. I didn't use it the following year because it wasn't the best approach for that group of learners. While many teachers contacted me about implementation and how they could make it work in their school, a handful were simply unable to do so due to class dynamics or crushing attitudes from other staff members. The message from this chapter isn't about the literal translation of 20 per cent time into your classroom. The message here is that teachers should be thinking about innovative ways to enhance learning and attitudes and trying them out without the fear of failure. It's not only about firing up your learners but about making them take learning seriously – helping them to care about it.

Take a risk and try something new – it will blow away the dust that forms on top of 'traditional' teaching. And, if it's genuinely done to improve, enhance or broaden learning, nobody can knock you for it.

TOP TIPS

- Remember to focus yourself several times throughout the day in the primary classroom. Ultimately, your job is about creating conditions in which children love learning.

- Talk to people. If it's all getting you down and you can't see a way out, spark up a conversation. Caretakers make great listeners (or, occasionally, great speakers).

- If you write down every single job that you 'must' do on a sticky note, trash any that have existed for longer than twenty-four hours.

Speak to Jonny's mum

Cover Miss Smith's breaktime duty

finish marking Y3's books

BEST BEFORE: TOMORROW

- Never let yourself forget that most of your class love you to bits. Don't let that 'one' incident blur your vision for anything more than a few hours.

- When you want to try something new, *do it*!

- Don't rush into things but, at the same time, don't waste so much time that you never become airborne.

- Be prepared for failure but, more importantly, be prepared to learn from it.

- There is no 'right' way to teach, so how can you go wrong?

- If no one tried out new things we would all be teaching exactly how the government expects us to. And everyone knows that is not effective or appropriate.

- If you implement any big changes, justify it to parents. If other staff members think you're a nutter, at least the parents will get why you're being a nutter towards their child.

- Don't let one child who doesn't like change stop you. Support them through the change because, ultimately, it's going to be better for everyone.

- If you have a spare Sunday afternoon, Stu has half a shed that needs painting.

Chapter 6

OZ TAKES CENTRE STAGE

Hell, there are no rules here – we are trying to accomplish something.

Thomas Edison

In a nutshell

In this chapter, Andy touches down in Sydney, we redraw a map of the world and discover that everyone is just a blue dot. We learn some lessons from the 1930s before bringing the chapter bang up to date with a discussion of computer games and apps in lessons. We finish with a comforting reminder that your mum is so proud of you, no matter what.

It was early morning as we touched down in Australia. Bleary eyed, I grabbed a taxi to a youth hostel and tucked into a bowl of corn-flakes and fresh milk. Three months in south-east Asia meant that a non-rice meal was greedily guzzled. Eventually, I removed my chin from the bowl and looked around. There was a huge world map on the wall. I did a double take. Australia was in the middle. How bizarre. The UK was still a tiny outcrop but shunting Oz to centre stage had moved us to top left, where America should be. And America had popped up on the right. I pondered that map for quite a while without realising I would end up writing about it thirty years later.

In the intervening period, the interweb was born. And the Google Maps app. For the uniniti-ated, you open the app and it tells you where you are. You are a blue dot. You can then tap in where you'd like to go and Google will plot a route and you can walk along, following the progress of the blue dot you. Rather like the Australians putting themselves in the centre of their world, the blue dot is how you live your life. You are, quite naturally, focused on yourself. Sure, you look out for others, but the world is processed and interpreted by you. You are the centre of your universe. And because of the way your mind works, you sort of assume that you are the centre of everybody else's universe too. But, of course, you're not. Everybody is their own blue dot, the epicentre of their own world.

we're all just little dots!

This has colossal implications. On a small scale, it means people really don't care if you're dancing like an idiot on the dance floor. They're not looking at you. In fact, the chances are, while you're feeling self-conscious, they're on their phones. It also means if you go to a conference and stand on your own, the whole world isn't actually looking at you. It feels like that's the case because you're focused on you, but they're very busy being focused on their own blue dot. It sounds a tad harsh, but nobody really cares that you're feeling self-conscious because they're all too busy feeling, guess what, self-conscious.

And on a much bigger scale, this has implications for teaching. Each child is their own blue dot. They have an identity, a self-image, some strengths and a whole load of insecurities running through their mind. The more you can find out about this blue dot, the better your chance of a positive relationship. And, as Rita Pierson says in her inspirational TED talk, 'Kids don't learn from people they don't like.'[1] So let's share a top tip before we even reach the end of the chapter. In fact two top tips. And these aren't just top teaching tips, these are top tips for life, coined by Dale Carnegie in his 1936 book, *How to Win Friends and Influence People*. First, be genuinely interested in the people around you. Obvious? Kind of. Easy to do when you have a class of thirty-five children? Not very. Carnegie's wisdom is to be *genuinely* interested, not lip service interested. And being genuinely interested in people takes time, effort and a considerable amount of emotional energy. But, to get into the world of the other blue dots, you have to be less interested in yourself and more interested in them.

And while we're on Mr Carnegie's train of thought, here's another belter that still holds true today: say nice things about people behind their back. We'd maybe go a bit further and advocate that you say nice things about them to their face as well, but Carnegie's tip is a sure-fire winner on two levels. First, if you say nice things about your pupils or work colleagues, it's likely that the school grapevine will whisper it back to them. And how morale boosting is it to hear that

1   Rita Pierson, Every Kid Needs a Champion, *TED* (May 2013). Available at: https://www.ted.com/talks/ rita_pierson_every_kid_needs_a_champion?language=en.

your teacher is praising you when you're not even there? *Whoosh!* The flames of a relationship! The second point is more technical. In psychology there is something that experts call 'spontaneous trait transference', which basically means that if you are saying nice things about someone, the person to whom you're saying nice things attributes those qualities to you. This is all done at a subconscious level, but I promise you that makes it more powerful rather than less. In a cutting edge chapter, we bring you advice from the, ahem, 1930s! Hey, we never said this would all be new stuff. But, my goodness, it's so very relevant in the modern world.

Bringing us into this millennium, the government, in their divine wisdom, have decided that 6-year-olds need to know what a noun phrase is and that 10-year-olds need to know how to use dashes for parenthesis and understand what a modal verb is. I did what most primary teachers did, I sighed and got on with it. But my focus was on how to breathe some life into this near-death diktat. True to form, it wasn't long before the free sample books of photocopiable worksheets poured through the school letterbox. Although they seemed a tempting option, I figured they were more likely to hasten the death knell of the English syllabus rather than be the miracle cure. I needed something to make the children actually care about all of this new grammar content, something to capture them in true primary school fashion. Perhaps some transparency is needed here too – if I'm totally honest, something to make *me* truly care about it was also required.

Then the realisation dawned. Children, along with those ridiculous cat videos on YouTube, love apps and games. So, playing to my advantage, I started a game of *Temple Run* on the class iPad. There wasn't much questioning going on as to what teacher actually thought he was doing striking up a game of *Temple Run* in the middle of a literacy session. In fact, to an outsider, it would appear almost natural and expected. Within minutes, the children were gathered around watching my poor attempt to outrun the pursuing evil monkeys and, after face-planting right into a tree, I posed one simple challenge to the class: 'Give me some verbs to describe what happened.'

It wasn't long before we had compiled a class list of thirty-two verbs, all with past, present and future variations. *Thirty-two!* I'd sort of expected ten and considered myself ambitious at that. Following on from this, we then looked at active and passive verbs, with equal excitement. It was almost surreal. Even I was ecstatic about verbs!

Thrilled with the results, we began the following day by playing the highly addictive *Angry Birds*, this time to check our understanding of speech marks and possessive apostrophes. For anyone unfamiliar, it's a simple yet complex (work that one out!) game where birds destroy strange green pigs by being catapulted through the air. The children wrote speech captions for the birds and the pigs utilising a whole array of punctuation and adventurous vocabulary – all the while fuelled by enthusiasm. You can imagine some of the things the children decided the birds would shout as they shot through the air at top speed! The children were competitive and consequently pushed their vocabulary choices to new limits. I began to plan all sorts of fiction and non-fiction writing based around the game too – discussion texts about whether to support the birds or the pigs, biographical writing about the birds, a newspaper account about the invasion of the pigs, a persuasive advert to download the app, and the list goes on.

We continued by learning about prepositions using *Cover Orange* (a puzzle game in which the player has to save oranges from being destroyed by covering them – aptly named!), and we looked at the rules of direct speech by using *Crazy Taxi* (a taxi-driving game that happens to be somewhat crazy). The latter was particularly fun as we considered what the passengers and/or pedestrians might be shouting following some of the children's driving. The direct speech suggested by certain colleagues is not repeatable nor suitable for a primary classroom. I suppose they were rather realistic though.

The learning was sustained throughout the weeks using games to punctuate bullet points and to model the use of hyphens to avoid ambiguity ('the man-eating pigs' was a particularly fun moment when we considered omitting the hyphen). It was all so fun, engaging and downright hilarious. And goodness only knows what it was like for the children!

I'm as guilty as any primary teacher: I've had evenings (fortunately not many) where I've spent a long time meticulously creating and preparing resources, hoping that they would grab the children's attention and breathe life into the lifeless syllabus. How foolish of me. Using these apps saved me loads of time and they were far better than anything that I could muster on a school night. The hard work was already done and I had the easy-peasy bit of, well, playing them. Suddenly, my lessons were looking modern, sprightly and engaging.

And you don't even need technology either (something that we touch on in the next chapter). A simple 'showdown' game worked well too. Put on some old Western music, stand the children back to back, teacher gives them a noun, children shout the type of noun followed by 'BANG!' and fire their opponent back to their seat. (Where they, of course, devise their revenge strategy.) This is just one example of turning even the most mundane of curriculum content into something a little more awesome. It's all very simple, probably something you've played around with before and, most importantly, you will see children genuinely excited about the prospect of grammar. They will even care more and more about it and, in another trick of the laws of the universe, you will have created an intrinsic desire to learn grammar. Forty years from now, your students will be doing what you do, idling away a ten day Eurocamping holiday in France spotting wrongly placed or missing apostrophes. Its' a funny old world.

I'm not painting a false picture that every lesson was a blast – oh no, not in the slightest! I'd still have those days where you question your career path because your life-changing plans have turned out to be time-wasting plans, but the mindset certainly sharpened things up. It refocused me on what really matters. And it made me fall that little bit more in love with teaching.

Try these ideas out. There are guys and girls out there doing this way better than me and they have some incredible ideas and teaching sequences. But with this book not telling you *what* to do, there has to be something more to this chapter, right? Yes!

So here's our big chapter ending – we all want to do great work and make our mum proud. And, believe me, your mum *is* proud. If you love what you do, your mum will be purring that you're brilliant at your job and she will be proud that you're doing something you adore. If you hate your job, your mum will be purring because you're the kind of person that does stuff they don't enjoy in order to take responsibility for earning a living for your family. You are a primary school teacher so, as far as your mum's concerned, you are a winner. But as far as your quality of life is concerned, only one of the above scenarios leaves you as a winner.

The brilliant teacher captures the children first and understands that everything else flows naturally from that. It's the oldest trick in the big book of obviousness. But to truly engage the children you have to find a way of loving what you do.

TOP TIPS

- Children don't learn from people they don't like. End of.

- If you're going to use an app to teach fractions, don't search for 'fractions apps'. Find something that excites the pupils and then work around that.

- Don't be afraid to play around on apps in your planning, preparation and assessment time. It can often be the foundation of a great project, particularly when colleagues get involved.

- Don't directly refer to your class as 'blue dots', but do remember that, even at such a young age, they have their own worries too. You might be terrified about a pending Ofsted visit, they might be worried if mum's doing carrots for tea.

- Be genuinely interested in people.

- Say nice things about people behind their back.

- Occasionally radicalise your classroom – try to get every child working with, and learning about, children they wouldn't normally touch with a barge pole. It makes a big difference to the ethic of the room.

- When you're all app-ed out, try getting children to change homophones in song titles. 'All You Knead Is Bread' has to be our all-time favourite Beatles effort.

- Your mum is so proud of you. Write her a letter telling her how grateful you are for all the things she's done for you. Send it (we dare you)!

Chapter 7
'BOOKS' AND 'COVERS'

Don't judge people by their outward appearance. Study their entrails.

Philip Ardagh

In a nutshell

In this chapter, Stu tells us about another of his train journeys and we learn two age-old lessons. Stu also harps on about dictionaries, outdoes Roald Dahl and makes a heartfelt apology to a random guy.

I spend very little of my life on trains. Yet here I am with a second train incident that changed my thoughts. (Note to self: maybe I should use trains more often.) This incident took place on a short journey in Norfolk with my wife and daughter, who was 7 months old at the time.

Outbound journey. Early morning. A smartly dressed businessman came and sat across from us. He sent a few emails and browsed a few websites on his smartphone and, only then, noticed us sitting opposite. Observing my daughter's slight restlessness at the time, he put a picture of his dog on the screen in an unenthusiastic bid to impress her. Not too uncharacteristically she didn't spark up much of a smile. The prospect of grabbing the phone and sampling its taste seemed mildly appealing, but rather impossible when the phone returned to its slavish email duties. Nevertheless, we all continued about our business and thought no more of it.

Return journey. Mid-afternoon. Far too many shopping bags yet one considerably happier wife. We ended up sitting facing quite the opposite sort of person. This guy was rough looking with a huge satchel that clanked with cans of Tennent's Extra every time he moved it. He sported a black knitted hat, an unshaven chin and heavy jowls. Tattoos oozed out of his sleeves. In-between shielding his smoker's cough, his callous hands hugged the coffee that he'd bought (presumably to temporarily sober him up before he opened his bag). His hollow eyes met with ours, which wasn't difficult given the 'directly opposite us' circumstances. He was the sort of guy that, if you'd met him in a dark alley, you'd just hand over your wallet without waiting to be asked.

Before I tell you, in proper *Question of Sport* style what happened next, I need to share some information about tiny human beings. Babies have what Zen Buddhists call 'original face'. They're not putting it on and they're not trying to be anyone else. They're not even trying to fit in. They don't have an ego and, bless 'em, they haven't learned to judge. They're just 'being'. By the time we inherit them in Key Stage 1, the 'learned self' has got a grip and by Key Stage 2, the human herding instinct has taken over and they have learned to conform.

But my nappy-clad little girl remained egoless and non-judgemental. So, guess what, she chose this train journey to seize the opportunity for human interaction. Despite our best possible distraction efforts she only went and smiled at Mr Tennent! That was it. No going back. My wife and I shared a nervous glance. The guy slowly raised his hand, revealing more tattoos, which I now assumed were all part of the same one that was creeping out of the neck of his t-shirt. He lowered his hand down onto the table and pretended to be a spider. *What the?* The hand scurried across the table as our daughter merrily tried to attack it – all with a huge grin spread across her chops. Her face was a picture![1] No matter how hard she tried, the spider was just way too quick! Forwards, backwards, sideways, sometimes scampering

---

1 They say that a picture is worth a thousand words. But, with all the funding cuts, it's worth about 378 now.

the length of the table, she absolutely loved it and, despite continuing for a good fifteen minutes, she never lost interest. Each time was just as hilarious as the first. Her squeals of delight had infected my wife and I. My face ached. People were leaning in and watching from neighbouring seats. The whole carriage had received an emotional uplift, courtesy of the amazing Mr Tennent (Tennent's 'Extra' he most certainly was).

At first glance, the messages in this story are that my daughter doesn't like dogs and we don't like unshaven guys with grubby fingers. Or (gulp!) about my terrible and unforgivable prejudices. But when you look closely there is a small reminder that what you have really doesn't matter. The businessman with his modern technology, fancy features and cute dog pictures was a let-down. The scruffy bloke with his spider hands was an absolute hoot. In short, it's about being your best self and going for it. I'm not sure what the dictionary definition of 'engagement' actually is but it was right here, right now, in my railway carriage.

Relating this story back to the classroom, impressive technology, futuristic classrooms and space age learning facilities are great extras, but none are as great as you. Or at least, you at your absolute engaging best. Too often in primary schools we blame a lack of, or outdated, resources. In fact, let me confess, I've moaned several times when the Internet has died or a projector bulb has blown. Suddenly, as the initial shock kicks in, I feel as though my teaching can't be effective and that we all need to go home. If the Internet is down, there is no point in human existence any more – random videos of cats cease to exist, children have to revert to using dictionaries and I can't enjoy the experience of the hundred or so emails that teachers seem to be subjected to daily. Yet, it's when you are put in these situations that you realise the power that the modern day teacher has and how very little said teacher actually needs. On the simplest of levels, a teacher needs a voice and perhaps somewhere to write. Have you ever given yourself one day a month (or a week if you're brave) when you use nothing other than your own voice and a whiteboard? Horrible at first, but exceptionally powerful in the end. And, when you think about it, it worked for us when we were at school, right?

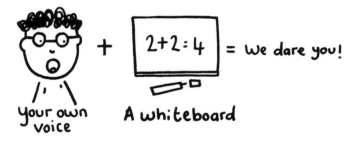

Your own voice + A whiteboard (2+2=4) = We dare you!

I mentioned reverting to dictionaries above, so for any reader who's baffled here's a small rant to explain. Think of this as 'the hidden chapter'. As someone who has a love of words (perhaps more than a love of academia), I think dictionaries are great for both historical significance and the exploration of new words. When I was 7, I sat down to read a dictionary and spent the rest of Year 3 trying to impress my teacher with the continual use of the word 'aardvark'. Needless to say, I didn't make it through the entire dictionary.

More recently I've had some interesting discussions with colleagues, fellow teachers and educators on the issue of dictionaries for spelling. It all started with a classroom situation, somewhat abridged for the sake of space.

Pupil: How do I spell Buckingham Palace? Oh, I'll get a dictionary. [Looks intently through dictionary] It's not in here.

Me: Google it?

Pupil: Okay.

You get the idea, but I want to keep this point short and sweet. By googling a word, the child:

♦ Attempted to spell the word to the best of their ability.

- Was presented with suggestions for an incorrectly spelled word.

- Received a list of search results to explore the word further.

- Gained access to thousands of images relating to the word (which also confirmed that they were barking up the right tree).

- Was likely to encounter further (or even serendipitous) learning from any intrigue resulting from the search results.

It is very important for me to emphasise at this point that I am not saying that we need to do away with the teaching of spelling. In fact, quite the opposite. Children need to learn spelling patterns, rules and guidelines as part of basic human life. The point I am trying to make is that we, as potentially brilliant teachers, need to appreciate and embrace the impact (and slant) that the Internet can add to spelling. You only have to speak to a handful of remotely technologically competent people to find that many of them will Google a word for the sake of ease, either for spelling or defining purposes.

What makes me proud is that, when it comes to spelling, children in my class naturally flutter between dictionaries and Google. They will often use the two in conjunction and it works an absolute treat. What's more, Google seems to be the more efficient option in terms of time and results – unless the child becomes distracted by the fourteen million results for 'penguin'. Children with dyslexia seem to benefit massively from it too – but that's a different discussion for a different day. You see what I'm saying? Don't be afraid to change your approach to suit the evolving world.

Where were we again? Trains! There is another huge message from my train experience that makes me shameful every time I remind myself that I went against it. The classic saying 'never judge a book by its cover' rings out here. I can't believe I judged the poor fella on his appearance. So, if the rough guy with the bag of beer, axes and *Cluedo*-style lead pipes is actually a teacher, and he's reading this, I'm sorry, dude! The spider trick was awesome! And here's the second message for all of you brilliant primary teachers: don't write anyone off. Ever. Don't permanently label any pupil, parent or staff member. No matter what the lock is, there is always a key. Even if that key is a metaphor for brute strength and destruction, there is always a way that the brilliant teacher will strive to find.

Remember there is always a KEY
※ Nevergiveup

Let me make the point even more starkly. Picture yourself in this scenario. It's a cold, bitter morning of semi-darkness and you're running late. You get into your car only to discover that it's severely frozen up. With the fans on full pelt, you frantically search around for the de-icer, only to discover that your partner's taken it. It's a deep frost and you've only got the scraper. You log it in your memory as something to complain about later. Cursing like a Tasmanian devil, you hack away for a minute or two and cut a small hole in the ice. It's exactly not-quite-big-enough-to-see-through but, hey, the roads are going to be icy and that slows the traffic, which means you're going to be late.

You belt up, lean forward so your nose is almost touching the small misted up hole and switch off the blaring radio. You're not entirely sure why you can't have the radio on when it's icy, but you've not got time to question this particular law of the universe. You crunch the car into gear and slide off the driveway without the foggiest idea of what is in front of you. Everything's fine until, *crack*, you drag your car against the wall and, within twenty-four hours, an insurance broker appears armed with a clipboard and neatly pressed trousers (he's wearing those, thankfully) and condemns your car. Writes it off completely. That's a pretty bad day. Bewildered by the whole experience, you wonder what the hell you're going to do now. Your plans have been scuppered and most people are just going to laugh at your stupidity. One small mistake and it's ended up costing you. And what a ridiculous over-reaction by the pressed trouser chap. You then spend the rest of the month trying to sort things out and catch up.

And that's how some children in school will feel. Are you the insurance broker teacher? Tough question. I'm not saying that this is done consciously but think carefully and honestly – have you ever written off a child as a lost cause? Have you ever lost energy and given up on a seemingly impossible battle? I'm sure you know the sort of child I mean. They're often falling asleep during guided reading because they were up most of the night playing *Call of Duty* (the 18 rating is just for fun, honestly mum!), and they know they'll get away without bringing their PE kit because nan's written them a note. There is a good chance that dad's gone mental at you in the past because you suggested that he might want to raise his expectations of his child. Oh, and mum keeps out of the way, except when she wants to have a moan about how crap the school is. The homework's too easy. Or too hard. There's not enough homework. There's too much homework. And despite having moved her darling child around seven different schools in the past three months, she can't quite put her finger on what the problem is. Hmm ...

The easy argument is that you can't teach someone who doesn't want to learn. So, let's gently remind you of the title of this book – it alludes to being a brilliant primary teacher. Not a giver-upper-on-seemingly-no-hopers teacher. And this is where it gets really tough. We're challenging you to find out why they don't want to learn and put an end to it. While you may not have parental support and while other teachers may tell you various stories about climbing a mountain with roller blades on, where's the proof that you can't actually make a difference? A big, massive, 'I'm gonna be an astronaut!' difference? It's just that the easy option is, well, easy. But being a *brilliant* primary teacher isn't about easy options.

Avoiding the easy route took me to the moon

Thinking inside the box

As a child, Zaphod had been diagnosed with ADHDDAAADHD (ntm) ABT which stood for Always Dreaming His Dopey Days Away, Also Attention Deficit Hyperflatulence Disorder (not to mention) A Bit Thick.

Douglas Adams, *The Hitchhiker's Guide to the Galaxy*

So how do you do it, eh? Intervention? So often we throw the word intervention around like a mythological weapon – and quite often rightly so because it's mostly effective. But if you're dealing with a lion that doesn't want to eat vegetables, you're not going to stick said lion in a greengrocers for a day. To get your lion fired up you'd be better off sticking it at the meat counter at Morrisons. You need to find something the disengaged child loves and use that to get them on your side for a start. Get to know that particular blue dot of a child and unearth their talents because these will form your army and lead you to victory. So the big question is, what is your challenging child's equivalent of the lion's meat feast? What kind of learning will make them drool in anticipation? Who says you can't teach volume with *Minecraft* blocks? Who says you can't teach adverbs with Lego dudes? And who's stopping you from writing instructions about 'crossing the fiery pit of doom' rather than how to make a sodding jam sandwich? And it's most definitely not at the expense of the rest of the class – chances are, they'll love it too!

Sadly, it's not just the children either. There is the writing off of staff members, parents and governors. Whether it's supporting a struggling teaching assistant or helping a fellow teacher get their head around modal verbs, once you choose to make a difference, you will. But it's got to start with that conscious choice and that strong belief that you will do it.

Thinking inside the box

Small print for the contract of 'Life'.*

* Available for a limited time only. Limit one (1) per person. Sell-by date, approx. 4,000 weeks after birth. Subject to change without notice. Non-transferrable and sole responsibility of the user. No warranty, even if misused by the owner. Additional parts sold separately. Terms and conditions apply. Best before: death.

Anon.

Let me get up-close and personal for a paragraph or two. When I first started teaching I took over a class mid-year. As luck would have it, I took over from one of the most talented teachers on this planet and, naturally, it wasn't really a walk in the park. Unless it was a barefoot walk and the park was full of hedgehogs. And hungry bears. Who could breathe fire.

There was one girl who took an instant dislike to me. I tried and tried to win her round but, being young and naive, I wasn't sure that I was getting anywhere. On the day she left school, her exact words to me were: 'You know what, Mr Spendlow? When you first started here I hated you. But you're alright actually. And I'll really miss you.' Gulp. It was at that point I made a vow to ensure that no child was ever written off. If a grumpy 11-year-old girl hadn't written me off, there was no way I was going to do it to any child.

To add Andy's spin, he reckons that every person on the planet has six significant talents, two of which become apparent very early, the next two are drawn out by awesome teachers and the final two are taken to the grave. What a waste of human flourishing. We believe your job is to uncover all six. Ken Robinson calls it 'the element'.[2] Scientists would call it the state of flow.

2 Ken Robinson with Lou Aronica, *The Element: How Finding Your Passion Changes Everything* (New York: Penguin Books, 2009).

It's that confluence between your natural aptitude and personal passion. Let me give you an example. One of my mates had a son who was a bit, how shall I put it, prone to attracting the attention of the senior management team. Let's call him a 'head teacher magnet' and his magnetism first reared its (magnetic) head in primary school.[3] In Year 5 he was caught selling sweets in the playground. He'd buy them from Asda and flog them at twice the price just before lunch when kids were at their hungriest. As an economist, I think it's pretty cool that he worked out the whole supply and demand thing and that he could maximise profits in that pre-lunch slot when reception kids were eating and the older ones were in the catering holding pen.

Roll UP. ROLL UP ← Is this possibly a young Sir Alan?

✻ Unlock the potential

---

3 Three 'magnets' in one sentence is fairly impressive but not as good as Roald Dahl's three 'violets' (look for the immortal line in *Charlie and the Chocolate Factory* of, 'Violet, you're turning violet, Violet').

Of course, the head didn't share my love of economics and the lad's tremendous business acumen was frowned on. His business was duly shut down, at least for a couple of weeks, before it reappeared at 3.30 p.m. outside the school gates. Our budding Alan Sugar (selling sweets, geddit?) continued to be frowned on with a similar fish 'n' chip ploy at big school with the head magnet eventually gathering enough pulling power to attract the local constabulary. The result was that, despite being bright as a supernova, the boy drifted through school and couldn't be bothered with the academic discipline of A levels. He tolerated it but school wasn't really for him. Six years on, he has a thriving Internet business buying and selling cars, earns more than your average head teacher and works three days a week. His magnetism has morphed and he's become a money magnet.

This true anecdote isn't meant to be a rant at the 'system' that did its utmost to extinguish this lad's sense of drive, leadership, entrepreneurialism, creativity and communication. Rather, it's aimed at highlighting the salience of Andy's six innate talents. Or maybe it's aimed at posing a bigger question: how could the school have served that child better? Or, an even bigger knee-shaker of a realisation-cum-question: if you had that child in your class, how could you identify and harness that talent?

And this is why teaching is less of a science and more of an art. Because the answer doesn't fit into a sentence or even a book. The answer lies within the relationship between teacher and student, and that's exactly where 'world class' lives. And, while inspectors may only care about the statistics of a child, primary teachers should care about shaping that child's life. Dig deep, work hard and find those talents because that's the greatest reward of them all.[4]

Thinking inside the box

Most of what you think is wrong with you is simply part of the human condition. You are faulty. So am I. Everybody has moods and down days. Everybody makes silly mistakes. Everybody has regrets. Everybody fails at some things. You are flawed. And if you spend your life focusing on all of the above you will be sad and insecure.

Good news. You are also a genius. You are the best you on the planet. You have had successes. You have had good days and serious

4 Except maybe a decent pension.

glee. You have done things you are immensely proud of. You have strengths and talents. On balance, I reckon that if you can focus on these points, then you'll have more energy and confidence, and you'll feel lucky.

Andy

TOP TIPS

◆ Know your weaknesses but don't build your life around them. Work out your six signature strengths and find opportunities to play to them. You will come alive.

◆ Speaking of which, there is a difference between 'being alive' and 'living'. The former is good news; the latter is life changing.

◆ If you're having a hard time with a pupil, remind yourself that they're young and still have a lot to learn. Part of your job is to nurture them. Talk to colleagues and try to find an answer – don't blame the under-12-year-old.

- When you feel like you've half-written off a pupil, work twice as hard to get them back.

- Don't judge a child by their parent (yes, we know this is a toughie).

- Spend time looking at what young children are into these days and work it into your teaching. It's just as important as researching 'how to teach inference to Year 1s'.

Chapter 8

AN APPLE FOR TEACHER?

Fun starter: show your Key Stage 2 class a fire door with the sign 'This door is alarmed'. Ask them to consider alternatives such as 'This window is baffled' or 'This floor is bewildered'. Just don't try it with a vending machine that is 'Out of order' – you will begin to uncover just how 'developed' your Year 4 children's vocabulary actually is.

In a nutshell

In a chapter of two halves, we kick off by making the case for calculated risks, we learn why Stuart loves courses, we dream of a Thames office and we learn to trust ourselves that little bit extra. Part two is more fruity as we learn about Stuart's Apple obsession, he gets a little bit 'if I ruled the world' with us all, we question why a 'new' curriculum doesn't get hyped at launch and we consider the message that our classroom, dress and mannerisms send out to heavily influenced primary children.

I absolutely love going on courses. Ten per cent of that love comes from the course content and what I'll be taking away from it in order to change the world. The remaining 90 per cent comes from meeting new people and listening to their tales, views and thoughts on their job. Half of the time it makes me thrilled or grateful to have the job that I do, and other times it fills me with jealousy, shock or admiration at what life is like for teachers across the country. This particular course was astonishing. I haven't got a clue what it was about …

There I met a woman who was a self-titled 'experienced teacher' who had maintained the same post for twelve years. I didn't question whether that was twelve years of experience or eleven repeats of one year of experience, but I did wonder in a cruelly judgemental way. Being young and perhaps a little too confident, I started banging on about how I loved taking risks in a bid to continually improve. She advised me, poker faced, that she had stuck to what she'd always done and that she didn't believe in taking risks. What's more she was from the school of 'if a job needs doing properly, do it yourself' and, as a result, she didn't trust anyone else to do things for her. Ouch! It seemed to me that her risk-free approach was, paradoxically, very risky indeed. The safety net of doing the same thing every year might be putting her entire existence at risk. Her job had become stale and mundane and it was etched in her eyes and her body language. It wasn't just a poker face she was wearing; it seemed to me that this teacher was clothed in the weight of the world.

Bravely, I asked about her day. She wasn't so keen when I pointed out that she'd taken a risk travelling by car and that she'd placed trust in the other five hundred motorists that she'd passed to remember how to drive safely and stick to it. She soured when I demonstrated how she'd trusted the bar staff to produce her coffee without mistakenly brewing tea and how she'd risked the fact that one disgruntled employee may find the need to poison it. The biscuit that she had half consumed seemed to be free of another delegate's poorly timed sneeze, but I did intimate that there was no guarantee. Her happiness didn't increase when I suggested that she was taking a risk that her class would survive without her as she'd placed huge trust in a supply teacher to manage the day. Then there is the course itself. How could she possibly trust the organisers and presenters to produce something that would help her better herself? Needless to say, she didn't touch the lunchtime buffet.

I'm not usually that awkward. Honestly. But she'd really irked me. How could a teacher possibly take that stance? How could a professional with such a responsibility claim to trust no one? And how could any effective teacher not take massive risks in order to better themselves? And the bizarre thing is that she started to laugh. She had fully got my point. Her tone of voice became softer and she unfolded her arms. The next ten minutes were life changing for us both. Life changing in a 'lesson learned' sort of way, not a horribly clichéd 'she jacked in her job and opened a cafe in a fishing village in Halkidiki' kind of way. She spoke for ages. And, for the first time in a while, I properly listened to her. The frostiness thawed (from both of us) and we began to share stories, experiences and barriers. In the interest of confidentiality and ethics, I'm going to omit a lot. But the message is there in all its importance.

It turns out that the damage had stemmed from her NQT year. As a young, somewhat care-free NQT at the age of 24, she had always pushed barriers, challenged the norm and attempted to be a new age education maverick. She thought that she could change the world, that nothing could stop her and that she would inspire generations. While she admitted that she probably needed bringing down a peg or two, nothing could have prepared her for the reality of what happened. Miraculously, I wanted to hug the ice queen.

Due to changing circumstances at the school where she worked, she had not been assigned a mentor as such. Several staff members dipped in and out of her professional career and she never kicked up a fuss because she assumed a breadth of ideas and input would surpass one single opinion. She had observations, observed others, kept a diary, reflected, had ups and downs. Then the massive downer reared itself like a bear with a sore head. A very grizzly head teacher.

This now almost tearful woman explained how she was called into the head's office and spoken at for quite some time. Apparently, other staff members felt threatened by the way that she did things and claimed that she was too much of a risk to standards. While there was nothing to back up these claims (supposedly – I have to take her word on this), the school had decided to take action by monitoring her extremely closely. Her life became miserable, stress became the norm and she began to become distant, not just from colleagues but her family too. She became an introvert who cared very much about children's education but was too afraid to make a difference. Standards did indeed drop and she eventually made the choice to move school and location.

She spent the next few years in a lovely school, doing what she needed to in order to keep people happy. Standards weren't exceptional but they were in no way poor. She felt content because the previously felt stress seemed a distant memory and she began to rebuild connections with her family. Another move came with a repeat of what worked – plodding gently along doing what others thought she should. She wasn't exactly happy but it worked. And then she went on this course …

Cutting a long personal story short, she told me to keep taking risks and never become crushed by scepticism. She explained that justification was essential and that no one should take risks that could have a long term negative impact on anyone's learning – something I could not agree with more. Finally, she explained that her past would never allow her to start taking big risks in her practice again, but she admired those who were able to do so. Heart wrenching stuff. This teacher could have been one of the biggest gurus in twenty-first century education. In fact, she was crushed, trapped and haunted. But what an amazing person to carry on with all of that pulling her back.

Thinking inside the box

I've missed more than 9,000 shots in my career. I've lost almost 300 games. 26 times I've been trusted to take the winning game shot and missed. I've failed over and over and over again in my life. And that is why I succeed.

Michael Jordan

Not only is this a poignant story but it also highlights the power of the human social instinct. Essentially, this teacher had learned to conform to what was 'okay'. Our noble profession had sought to knock the inspirational risk taking edges off her so that she could sink into 'mundane' where, sadly, she would fit in and feel more comfortable.

This next passage is a tough one so we put our heads together: we've rewritten it several times in an attempt to convey what we mean without it sounding like we're having a go. Have you ever experienced a new member of staff who is full of energy and excitement and thought, that will never last? Because, if so, you could be part of a staffroom culture where, subconsciously, you are part of the dampening down of enthusiasm. We said at the outset that we want you to be the leading light of your staffroom. We want you to be the one full of energy and unbridled passion for teaching, the one who speaks highly of your profession in the pub on a Saturday night, the one full of optimism about what children can achieve and, consequently, when the new classes are announced, the one the kids rush home to talk about: 'Guess what mum, I've got Miss So-and-So next year. Woohoo!'

Yes, we know it's difficult. And that's exactly the point! Mediocrity is so easy and safety so inviting. Awesomeness, *for thirty years*, is massive! We're back to the point that nobody gets out of bed with the determination to have a stinker of a day. Taking a benevolent view of the teaching profession, none of us wants to be a bad teacher. We all turn up wanting to do our very best, and it's often the system that gets in our way. Most teachers concur that 'teaching' is the best bit of the job but, in the highly politicised educational world, it often feels as though the teaching bit is becoming a smaller and smaller part of the overall package. Sometimes it's hard to be inspirational and take risks when the stakes are so damned high. You end up playing it safe.

Let us make a point that seems to escape most people – and on first reading, it's going to sound harsh. The 'system' of Ofsted, syllabuses, schemes of work, lesson plans, tracking, grading, job descriptions, colour-coded assessment and other paraphernalia and shenanigans – it's all in place to stop rubbish teachers being rubbish. It's all invented by somebody with a very big Thames view office in London who doesn't trust teachers because a few really bad ones will make headline news in the *Daily Mail*, and their comfy chair and Thames view will be gone. So they invent a near watertight system where everything is metaphorically bolted to the floor. If everything is tracked and monitored very little can go wrong. And, if it does go wrong, they have evidence so they can catch you! If you were in their job, you'd probably do the same. The unintentional by-product of the watertight system is that it stifles innovation. Not in an overt 'You aren't allowed to innovate' kind of way (because, in a bizarre twist of irony, the person with the river view would love you to inspire the kids and try new stuff), but more in a 'Keeping you so busy with peripheral system stuff that you haven't got the time or energy to innovate' kind of way.

The top people want to know exactly what you're doing and how you're doing it. And here's the syllabus and some lofty targets. They want it planned to the nth degree because that is least risky to them. And here *we* are, at classroom level, advocating that you go for it. What we're really, really getting at is the need not only to take risks but also to be confident in justifying them. Be heavily self-critical but do not fear risk. We take so many risks each day without realising it – what difference will a few more make? There has been no discovery of a 'perfect one-size-fits-all teacher', yet, so what's the point in not even bothering to explore a little? The system is there because it doesn't trust you. And that's a real pain to get your head around. But you have to get over it and be determined to shine *within* a structure that's not conducive to shining. Think of yourself as a glow-worm. They don't wait for the light – they create it! And if you know the glow-worm song, they're never glum ('cause how can you be grumpy when the sun shines out of your bum?').

Sorry, that sounded rather flippant. Here it is un-flippanted. The system doesn't trust you? We say, sod it. Trust yourself, take a few calculated gambles and be brilliant.

It's rather like personal branding. You will have certain brands that you like; we're guessing because they're sexy, exciting or imply top-notch quality. Anyone who knows Stu will know that saying he's an Apple fan is an understatement. He happily acknowledges this …

Apple could literally bring out an overpriced bottle of tap water and I'd jump straight at it armed with a debit card and a manic grin. It's not just the quality of their products, it's the whole package – the simplicity, packaging, quality, marketing and ethos. Every single move that they make is considered carefully and each and every word used in advertising a product is chosen precisely to have a specific effect on the consumer. There are some highly skilled word-smiths employed to make every aspect of every product sound unique, desirable and essential. So, their overpriced tap water wouldn't just be known as water. It would be described as a 'distinctive blend of both hydrogen and water atoms combined through a natural fusion process in order to produce a product that not only has molecular precision, but also feels natural to the human body'. To some people, it's known as 'bullshit'. I get that. To me, though, it shows care and effort. It's a strong message that very often brings high levels of exhilaration to a product launch. When a new product is released, the stores open at midnight to accommodate the stampede of Apple devotees.

Contrast that with education which is, to be fair, possibly *the* most important 'product' you will ever consume. In fact, let's be more specific and look at just one aspect of education: the launch of a new curriculum. When a new curriculum comes out (which, sure as the sun rises in the east, it will) there just doesn't seem to be that much excitement. There's not the hyped up arrival, the promotional material, an enthusiasm fuelled army of teachers fighting … erm, forming … an orderly queue to get their hands on it. Nobody downloads it at midnight. From networking with teachers on Twitter, I can conclude that the exact opposite takes place. It's a sort of bland heavy-heartedness of, 'Well, it's here, but we haven't got a bloody clue what we're going to do with it yet.' I liken the feeling to a childhood experience of being told by teachers for weeks that a 'really important' guest would be coming to school and, when the day finally arrived, and the local mayor turned up, I spent the whole day a little bit miffed that it wasn't Spider-Man.

Surely, the one thing you would do if you were launching a brand new national curriculum would be to muster up a bit of unbridled excitement. You'd want to get teachers champing at the bit, right? We appreciate that the government isn't Apple but with your one opportunity to make a huge difference to education you'd do something a bit extraordinary – maybe even radical. We like Richard Gerver's notion that what we have to do is make school feel like Disneyland,[1] which at face value is bonkers. Or is it? We think that is exactly the level of thinking that will get teachers to rise to the challenge. If the government can't begin to fathom it, and the majority of primary teachers baulk at its Disney glibness, then it's down to you to give it some consideration. And we don't think Gerver is advocating that you build a roller-coaster on your playground (although Andy knows him very well and wouldn't put it past him), but he is most definitely suggesting that the rules of engagement have changed.

The release of a new curriculum should lend itself to the opening of doors and for teachers all over the country to take a huge refreshing look at the job they do. Perhaps to find better ways of working. Perhaps to consider how they are going to work most effectively. In reality,

---

1 Richard Gerver, *Creating Tomorrow's Schools Today: Education – Our Children – Their Futures* (London: Continuum, 2010).

let's consider what actually happens. It's worth noting that this is not representative of all schools, but it has certainly rung out from speaking to colleagues, friends and other professionals across the country. The 'new' curriculum is released and many leave it well alone, instead focusing on what matters at the time: writing reports, organising sports day, casting the school play, eradicating that weird summer sickness bug that homes in around June time (often confused with knackeredness). Some folk with either a lot of free time on their hands, or a burning desire to hit the ground running with the new curriculum, start to cross-compare new and old. Some people jump straight to the 'bits I need to cover' parts and start to draw up plans of simply 'getting through it all' – completely missing the purpose and reasoning behind the new curriculum in the first place. Those that do read the aims and purpose of it realise that they are fighting a dangerous and complicated battle with the rest of the education world. Even some consultants become tangled in a bitter dispute over purpose.

While most of us would love to write a curriculum ourselves – putting energy and time into perfecting it, trialling it, developing it and then spreading the gospel through the world like a new-found religion, that just ain't gonna happen. It frustrates me as to why something as life changing and gigantic as a new curriculum doesn't have a grand launch and exciting atmosphere. Instead, it's a spry announcement, lots of drafts and then a final product – that doesn't actually exist in a physical form either.

Unfortunately, we can't do much about the lacklustre curriculum launch but what we can do is start to get that exuberant Apple-esque message and ethos into our classrooms. Because here is one of the biggest messages of all. We are all seduced by branding. We each have our favourite foods, clothes, gadgets and restaurant chains. Children are influenced by branding too – research by the University of Michigan in 2010 found that pre-school children recognised the McDonald's golden arches before they could actually read.[2] Primary aged children are so heavily influenced by what is around them because their behaviour is learned from peers and role models. Their habits, their speech, their attitudes and even their values are influenced by what goes on during those primary school years.

---

2   Anna R. McAlister and T. Bettina Cornwell, Children's Brand Symbolism Understanding: Links to Theory of Mind and Executive Functioning, *Psychology & Marketing* 27(3) (2010): 203–228.

We'd like to make the case that you are also a brand. How you look and sound creates a feeling in your customers. What's your packaging? What's your message? Why should your customers buy into you?

TOP TIPS

- Take some risks. When something goes awry ask yourself, 'Where is this issue on a scale of 1 to 10?' (where 10 is 'time to hand my notice in').

- Think about the message that your classroom emits. Maybe be *really* brave and ask others for their opinions.

- Does your appearance (your personal branding) reflect the way that you teach? While a teacher with frazzled hair and tattered clothes is going to look very busy, it doesn't reflect well on their own quality standards. (Harsh but true.)

- What makes you different to any other teacher in your school? Is there one skill or talent that makes you a worthy member of the team?

- What would be the three key elements of your 'logo'? A wine glass, panda eyes and a packet of ibuprofen? Better if you aimed for a smile, a light bulb and an image of you jumping in the air clicking your heels.

- Always make sure that you follow the example of the dragonfly – agile, remarkable and demonstrating incredible vision. Never be the slug – slow moving and leaving a trail behind for others to clear up.

Chapter 9

THE GOOD OLD DAYS

Schoolteachers are not fully appreciated
by parents, until it rains all day Saturday.

E. C. McKenzie

In a nutshell

In a humdinger of a final chapter, we learn stuff
we already know but don't necessarily put into
practice, Stuart shares some rules that you can
introduce to your twilight meetings and, best
of all, we give you some magic numbers that
will create wonderful relationships. We touch
on fixed and growth mindsets before popping
into NASA, proving that positivity is contagious, before finishing with a reflection on the
good old days.

We mentioned previously how we're pretty terrible at celebrating what we do well. Teachers,
on the whole, never stop and say, 'Well, that

157

was a totally amazing lesson, wasn't it!' because that's just not what we do. It's almost frowned on – one of those unwritten rules that everybody knows you never, ever mention. Bursting into the staffroom bragging about how awesome you are is just not the British way. And even if you have done something well, there simply isn't time to bask in the glory because there is something major just around the corner. Or there is a form to fill in. Or some data to analyse. Or a child with a bumped head. And no plimsolls.

Some of the most valuable staff meetings of my life have been the serendipitous ones where we end up discussing everyday teaching. There is this weird secret belief in some schools that teaching can only improve by going on a course or speaking to an 'expert'. And, of course, an expert isn't anyone who works within the school. I've learned some good tips and tricks from courses, but most of the good, long term, 'this is effective' stuff about teaching came from colleagues. So, I've taken to starting after-school meetings with the assertion of these three basic assumptions:

1 Assume everyone in this room is here to serve the greater good.

2 Given the above, assume nobody has any hidden agendas.

3 Given the above, assume we're all reasonable, even when we disagree, until proven otherwise.

It makes for in-ter-es-ting (pronounced as a James Bond bad guy would say it) meetings. Anyway, back to our non-agenda-ed gatherings – from these we all take ideas, ways to broaden our practice and a feeling that 'we're not in this alone'. They're absolutely brilliant because they're so practical, so realistic and so incredibly rich. But what happens when we've had one of these meetings? Everyone feels a little sheep-ish. A little bit like naughty schoolchildren who've got away without completing the main activity. A little bit like we shouldn't have done it because staff meetings must have a long term focus or huge end goal of bettering ourselves (despite being knackered from a long day/week/month/term – delete as appropriate). For people who spend most writing sessions reminding children, 'You've got to be able to talk it through before you can even begin to write it', we feel very, very hypocritical.

Thinking inside the box↘

Q. If you're caught in a trap, what's the one thing you have to do before you can escape?

A. You have to realise that you've been caught in a trap!

Jamie Smart

During teacher training, student teachers are encouraged to be self-reflective and use reflection to broaden their skills and, in turn, become better beings. The trouble is, there seems to be an almost unwritten rule that 'being reflective' must involve being critical and looking at how to make things better next time. And there is nothing wrong with that at all. I'll happily be the first to confess that I do everything with a mindset of improving it, scrapping it, altering it or strengthening it next time (the second edition of this book will be great). And that's where I see teachers going wrong. Well, everyone actually.

Once again, in an attempt to give a light and entertaining touch, I won't dwell on the dawn of human civilisation, merely allude to it and, in true British style, blame our current negativity on our ancestors. Have you noticed how it's always someone else's fault? Well, in this case, it really is. Those damned Neolithics with their primitive frontal lobes. You see, back in the day, life was very dangerous indeed and humans evolved through being cautious. All those happy-clappy risk takers who skipped around joyfully got picked off by the sabre-toothed tigers. Only the ultra-cautious ones survived. 'Don't eat this.' 'Don't, whatever you do, go in that cave.' 'Don't go out in the cold.' 'Don't wander into the forest.' You get the point. A wary mindset is what got us here today so, in a way, we should thank our negative ancestors. However, despite what the media might imply, the world is mostly nice and safe, yet our brains haven't kept up. We're still primed for danger.

Have you ever wondered why you like to climb big hills? It's so you can see for miles which, in the olden days, was useful in terms of spotting marauding enemies from afar. And why do you feel compelled to eat everything on your plate? Because, in the olden days, you didn't know when your next meal would be. So, in our house, the evening meal resembles the Stone Age as we all tuck in greedily and heartily (grunt grunt, nom nom), on the basis of the underlying

Homo erectus mantra that the first one to finish gets seconds and the last one gets none, so will die. Our brains cause us to conveniently forget that the cupboards are stacked and Sainsbury's Local is open till 11 p.m.

What I'm basically saying is that teachers are humans (whatever the *Daily Mail* says) and humans are pre-programmed to be negative. We scan the environment looking for danger. It's just the way we've evolved. That's why one awkward parent ruins your parents' evening and your brain somehow contrives to delete the twenty-nine who said, *to your face*, that you're awesome. One kid with attitude spoils your entire morning because you miraculously delete the twenty-nine cherubs. The one person cutting you up on the way home is the one you're still chuntering about as you stick your key in the front door. I rest my case.

When reflecting on your lessons, it is therefore the negative that weighs most heavily. So, what can you do about it? Well, the first thing is to be aware of it. And to counterbalance the evolutionary fact that negative weighs more than positive, you have to accentuate the positive. Not in a ridiculous Pollyanna-ish, 'Oooh, I can't wait for tomorrow's Ofsted visit. What a jolly jape it's sure to be!' kind of way. We're assuming you want some friends in the staffroom. But we dare you to push it to, 'Ofsted are in tomoz. Let's knock the socks off the bastards or, if not, we'll let Connor from Year 4 joyride their Mercedes!'

At an individual lesson level that means that you should spend time reflecting on what was amazing. There is a law of positive to negative – a ratio of 2.9301:1 – that's called the Losada principle. Rounding up, that means there has to be three positives for every negative. So, at the end of your day (or week) write/say three things that have gone remarkably well and one thing that you will do better next time. Not only will it retrain your brain to accentuate the positive, it's also an important factor outside the classroom. Three positives for every negative is the bare minimum for a relationship to survive. So, if I was a fly on the wall in your staffroom, I'd expect to hear at least three positive comments for every whinge. Ditto for after-school meetings – they need to be couched in positive language. Please note: it's not three to none. Losada doesn't mean you can't be negative, just that you need to be going out of your way to notice good stuff and commenting positively. And three positives to every negative is the bare minimum so, for example, if your marriage dips below the magic ratio it will struggle. High performance teams have a ratio of five to one. That means high performance staffrooms are a hive of positivity, praise and laughter. In the classroom, the ratio rises to a heady eight to one.

That means you have to go out of your way to catch your teaching assistant and the kids doing brilliant stuff, with wiggle room for the occasional negative. We're not saying this is fair and we're absolutely not saying it should be an excuse to spoon-feed false praise. Children know when they're being conned and, by and large, they don't want or expect praise if it's not warranted. But heed this: go out of your way to catch your children and fellow staff members doing good stuff, *and bloody well tell them!* Primary children seem to home in on and respond to this far better than anyone else too. If the environment around them is positive, how can the learning be anything other?

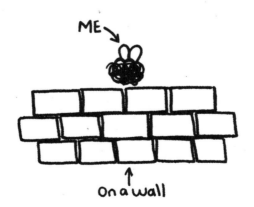

ME

On a wall

Current best practice, and common sense, is always go out of your way to praise for effort rather than talent. This chimes with Carol Dweck's work on fixed and growth mindsets[1] which you will almost certainly have had an INSET day about. To bastardise her amazing work into two short paragraphs, Dweck distinguishes between what she calls fixed and growth mindsets. Fixed mindset children tend to think that ability is solidified, so 'If I'm rubbish at English, I'll always be rubbish at English', which has the painful side effect that they give up when the going gets tough. These are the kids who pay lip service to the subject and then slump into their chairs grumbling that it's too hard. Or proving themselves right by failing at the first hurdle and basking in their failure by cheerfully announcing, 'I told you I couldn't do it, Miss.'

The opposite is a growth mindset. This is to be encouraged because it comes from the starting point that 'anything is possible if I apply myself'. These are the children who persevere when the going gets tough and, hey presto, in a self-fulfilling parallel universe, they end up achieving more than the giver-uppers. And Dweck's rather snazzy conclusion is that you can encourage growth mindsets by praising effort. So, if one of the children in your class manages to

---

1 Carol S. Dweck, *Mindset: The New Psychology of Success* (New York: Random House, 2006).

achieve something magnificent in story writing, it isn't, 'Nice one, Grace, you are destined to be the next J. K. Rowling' (i.e. talent), it's 'Grab yourself a star, Grace, and as you're sticking it on the chart, remind yourself how awesome you are when you put maximum effort into your work' (i.e. effort).

Like I say, it's one of those 'it's so obvious, why didn't we see it sooner?' pieces of research. And, it goes without saying that this *must* apply to your own kids and yourself too (but we thought we'd say it anyway!).

Thinking inside the box

Here are two short quizzes. You don't have to actually answer the questions – just ponder on them.

1 Name the five wealthiest people in the world.

2 Name the last five Grand National winners.

3 Name ten people who have won the Nobel or Pulitzer Prize.

4 Name the last half dozen Academy Award winners for best actor and actress.

5 Name the last six prime ministers.

Here's another five questions:

1 List three teachers who inspired you.

2 Name three friends who would stand by you no matter what.

3 Name five people who have taught you something worthwhile.

4 Think of a few people who have made you feel appreciated and special.

5 Think of five people you enjoy spending time with.

The people who make a difference in your life are not necessarily the ones with the most credentials, the most money or the most awards. They are often the ones who care the most.

So, here we are, the final bit of our book and time for some reflection of our own. We've tried to avoid any clever-dickery (although three variations of 'magnets' in one sentence is a bit dicky) and merely plant a few seeds of suggestion. Plus, we've tried to avoid too much ranty political stuff. However it may seem, we doubt that any secretary of state for education has ever *deliberately* set out to harm teachers or kids. It's all just political fall-out. The pig's bladder of education has been kicked about, muddied and, to push what started out as a promising metaphor just a little too far, the whole game has been refereed very badly. We haven't even argued that education is sooooo important that it should be taken out of politics altogether and run by an independent professional body of, dare we say it, teachers, who have a long term plan and vision. That really would upset that person with the Thames view.

We don't think people are against change per se. But we do think people are against change that is imposed and for which there seems no rhyme nor reason. But, hey, the whole tone of this book is to quit waiting. If we have 4,000 weeks on this earth then there isn't time to sit around waiting for a 'nice' education secretary, or for Ofsted to be disbanded, or for the standard of parenting to improve, or for everyone in the staffroom to bloody well cheer up. The revolution starts here with you. No pressure!

you've got just 4,000 weeks here!

#DoSomething!

We wanted to add a subheading to this book, a bastardisation of a Bill Clinton classic, 'It's all about the people, stupid!' which, in our game, of course, it absolutely is. So, let's tidy up a few loose ends.

A rainy evening in early September signifies something tragic. A tsunami of negativity, regret and misery gushes its way across social media as teachers prepare for their return to work. For most, they've more than likely spent the entire summer endlessly preparing due to a lack of prioritising what actually matters, which makes you wonder why they're so bothered about their imminent return to the classroom. And, of course, not only have they been working unnecessarily but they're also knackered before they've even properly started.

The following day is the dreaded moment. Countdown to half-term begins, sales of salad increase because everyone seems to be on some kind of token post-summer diet and school car parks gradually begin to fill as teachers make their way into school. There is an action packed year ahead of planning, marking, assessment, head lice, meetings, scrutinies, observations, angry parents, report writing, Christmas productions, parents' evenings, staff meetings and playground duties. Then there's the teaching bit too.

We don't need to spell out that we're being cynical. But what genuinely forms tears in our eyes is the negativity that seems to encompass a new academic year. And most of the given reasons are self-inflicted. People who can't say no, people who can't be effective until a learning objective has been written and read by all, people who half-fill glasses on Mondays and people who paint sheds in their entirety.

Further investigation and research reveals that life is absolutely jam-packed with negativity – we've already told you that a hundred times. So, it's not really a surprise that teaching is a career bursting with it too. Negativity is easy. Spark up a conversation about 'British weather' and you will have an army of gloomy minions all creating heaps more negative energy. An inherent British problem is that we tend to lower our expectations of what life could be. The result is that most people get stuck in what we call a C+ life. In school report terms, you 'could do better' and, for many, life can become a bit mundane. The solution isn't to lower your sights. In fact, we'd argue the opposite. Too many people settle for C+ in the hope that A* will happen at the weekend, or next year, or when they retire. It's almost as though we set out to expect mediocrity in the hope that something good might happen and surprise us. Accepting mediocrity is a defence mechanism because you will rarely be disappointed, but you will also rarely be genuinely happy.

Aim to make every day an A* day

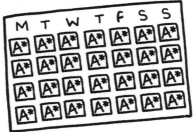

The solution is what we call 'realistic optimism'. Not some rose-tinted approach that annoys people and papers over the cracks of reality, but a genuine expectation that today is going to be a fab day because you're going to choose to be upbeat, passionate and positive. In a spooky *Matrix*-style psychological shift of mindset, you are more likely to have a fabulous day. The downside is that, despite your best efforts, the risk (there's that word again!) is the day might still conspire against you and you might be disappointed. But, hey, tomorrow you go for it again … What is that rubbish about only living once? We live every single day!

My therapist told me the way to achieve true inner peace is to finish what I start. So far I've finished two bags of M&M's and a chocolate cake. I feel better already.

Dave Barry

The chances are you're living life fast, but are you living it well? Stress related illness is at an all-time high. In 2013, 53 million antidepressant prescriptions were issued in England for people who needed help in feeling good, and the bad news is that your 'busyness' isn't going to go away. So what can you do? Well, a good place to start would be to take some of the lessons from this book and apply them. And, of course, you can continue to look externally for things that will make you happier and reduce your stress – handbags, shoes, football, beer, golf, sunbeds, Prozac and gin. Or, you could do what happy people do and look internally. Because the long term solution to happiness and flourishing lies within (if this were an audio book, it would blare out 'Hallelujah!' for a few minutes right now).

Of course, it's easier to feel great if you're doing a job you love. Whether you're engaged in your work depends on whether you view it as a job, a career or a calling. If, for you, teaching is a job, you will feel it in the pit of your stomach. Going to work will be a chore. You're doing it because it pays the bills and you get that feeling of angst when the alarm goes off at stupid o'clock. If, for you, teaching is a career, it's still a necessity but you see opportunities for success and advancement. It's up the evolutionary scale from a job and you're likely to feel you're moving in the right direction. You're invested in your work and want to do well. If, for you, teaching is a calling then the work is an end in itself. You will feel fulfilled and have a sense of contribution to the greater good. Work is likely to draw on your personal strengths and gives your life meaning and purpose. And, whisper it quietly, you'd probably do it for free.

Whether you're engaged in a job, a career or a calling has less to do with your work than you might imagine. A calling can have just as much to do with your mindset as it does with the actual work being done. So, let us remind you of the classic story of the man who was sweeping the floor at NASA. When someone asked him what his job was, he replied, 'I'm helping put a man on the moon.' Now, you might be lucky. Teaching might have beckoned you from afar. You knew you were destined to be a teacher from age 12 and you adore it. It's your moon landing and you are filled with daily joy. Teaching is your calling. Hurrah! But, for the majority, we have to put a modicum of effort into creating positive feelings from within.

Did you say 'effort'?

Yup, 'fraid so.

I'm already knackered. Why should I bother?

What, apart from the obvious argument that life's too short? If that's not reason enough, consider this: the first (and only) rule of influence is that you already have it. The key with influence is not therefore to acquire it; it's to appreciate that you've already got it and then expand and use it for the greater good. We've said this in other books before but it's so good we'll say it again: your happiness has a ripple effect, reaching people three degrees removed from you. This is our final piece of science and we reckon we might have saved the best to last. Happiness spreads via 'mirror neurons'. These are brain receptors that allow us to understand and mimic other people's emotions (note, these are often defunct in autistic people, hence their inability to empathise). Nick Christakis and James Fowler studied emotional contagion.[2] They did some mathematical analysis of social networks and found some magic numbers: 15 per cent, 10 per cent and 6 per cent. They discovered that, when you're upbeat, anyone who comes into direct contact with you is automatically 15 per cent happier, simply because they catch your positivity. I mean, that's a pretty cool notion, but it doesn't stop there. The person who you've elevated by 15 per cent impacts on the next person they meet, raising the second person's happiness by 10 per cent. And, in turn,

2   Nicholas Christakis and James Fowler, *Connected: The Surprising Power of Our Social Networks and How They Shape Our Lives* (New York: Little, Brown and Co., 2009).

this 10 per cent happier person impacts positively on the third person by 6 per cent. In your job, this is massive! Potentially, you are directly affecting hundreds of people each day, raising their happiness by at least 15 per cent. The kids go home 15 per cent happier, raising their parents' and grandparents' happiness by 10 per cent, raising the street's happiness by 6 per cent. We think this must, somewhere and somehow, equate to fewer 'angry parents' too ('I had a great day at school today, mum, and although I had to stay in at playtime to finish my science work, I did see the importance and the need for me to complete said science work, so there's really no need for you to kick up a fuss …').

Happiness is contagious

An interesting corollary, in terms of families, is that the strongest emotional path is from daughters to both parents. But, conversely, the parents' emotional states have very little impact on daughters. Fathers' emotions affect their partner and son, but less so their daughter. Emotions are especially contagious when fathers come home from work in a lousy mood – it makes the whole household miserable (except the daughters, who seem immune!).[3] And, in a note of caution for your own home life, how you come through the door is crucial. Children are much better off with parents who work long hours but love their job than parents who work shorter hours in jobs they hate.

Negativity is also very contagious. The statistic seems less certain but it appears that every unhappy person you come into contact with reduces your own happiness by 7 per cent. If your staffroom is inhabited by negative people, your job will be doubly draining.

Thinking inside the box

Be accountable. Live an interesting life. No one wants to talk to an old person with no stories to tell.

---

3   See Bruce E. Compas, David C. Howell, Normand Ledoux, Vicky Phares and Rebecca A. Williams, Parent and Child Stress and Symptoms: An Integrative Analysis, *Developmental Psychology* 25(4) (1989): 550–559; Reed Larson and Maryse H. Richards, *Divergent Realities: The Emotional Lives of Mothers, Fathers, and Adolescents* (New York: HarperCollins, 1994).

The biggest takeaways from Andy's area of research are that 'choice' and 'effort' are key factors in British happiness. We are culturally indoctrinated into a slightly doom and gloom dourness (which manifests in our favourite pastime of 'having a bit of a moan'). Boiling it down to the bare bones, what he's saying is that most people are a million miles away from feeling as great as they could. But, if you take account of emotional contagion, the effort taken to be your best self is repaid with massive interest – not only will it enhance your life but it will also provide an uplift for people you haven't even met.

We don't want to end on a downer but we reckon you've already realised that the ageing process is inevitable. You can look after yourself, go to the gym, eat healthy food, moisturise and take cod liver oil supplements but, ultimately, those birthday cards will have bigger numbers on them year by year. The days are relentless. But what if it isn't about vitamins and Nivea? What if the secret of eternal youth was in our heads – more specifically our *thinking* – and we could maintain some of that youthful, carefree exuberance that young children manage to generate? They're not fussed about the news. (To be fair, they don't have the same responsibilities of career, money, mortgage, bills, looking after poorly relatives and so on. No wonder Key Stage 1s are so effing happy!)

As we go through life we accumulate experiences and add layers of who we think we should be. We're striving to be a good parent, good teacher, good partner, good lover and good carer, while also keeping on top of our emails. There is a certain etiquette about how we think we should behave in certain situations. And, to be frank, life can get a bit serious. We become mummified under layers and layers of who we think we're supposed to be. But what if all those layers means we sometimes forget who we *really* are? What if your to-do list has so many things on it that you've forgotten your to-be list? What if we all have that youthful abundance bubbling inside but it simply gets covered over? And, therefore, what if the secret to eternal happiness isn't to learn a whole load of new stuff? What if the secret to being our best self is to peel back some of the layers to reveal who we truly are when we're being our best self? It's more than self-improvement. We call it self-remembering. And, hey presto, you are already a brilliant teacher (isn't that where we came in?), it's just that sometimes you forget!

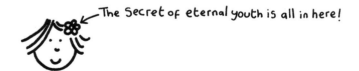

The Secret of eternal youth is all in here!

We're hoping that our book has acted as a simple reminder. And if you'll allow us one more pithy quote, after the making of *Jaws 4*, Michael Caine revelled in its awfulness saying, 'I have never seen it. But by all accounts it is terrible. However, I have seen the house that it built, and it is terrific!'

We appreciate that life is a short and precious gift, so we sincerely hope we haven't made you endure anything quite like *Jaws 4*. Just so you know, writers rarely get rich. Our aim is more lofty than accruing wads of cash. Stu, a proper hands-on day-to-day teacher, sees colleagues struggling with ever increasing workloads. Andy, a regular school speaker, meets hundreds of awesome human beings who are being eroded by the system, counting down the number of sleeps until their next half-term. We care like hell. So, hand on heart, we can safely say that we've written *The Art of Being a Brilliant Primary Teacher* with the very best of intentions. And, as always, it's very simple: we hope to make some sort of positive difference to primary teachers across the land.

Thank you for reading.

POSTSCRIPT

Thinking inside the box

You cannot be anything you want to be – but you can be a lot more of who you already are.

Tom Rath

It's Boxing Day at Andy's house and Dave and his family are popping round from next door …

I chatted to the kids and convinced them that it would be a wonderful idea to get Dave's backside into our positive chair. 'He's the biggest energy vampire in town,' I reminded them. So here's the challenge. Would the chair work if the person sitting in it didn't know it was a positive chair? We reflected on the previous month. The positive chair had worked 100 per cent of the time. 'Even on grandma,' Ollie reminded us, still sounding a little surprised. But everyone who had sat in it had already been told it was a positive chair. Would the chair work if they didn't know? We fist-bumped. It was game on. Dave was due at 11 a.m.

The POSITIVE chair

Looks just like a normal chair, feels like Something totally different!

It was one of those strange mornings when the time between breakfast and 11 a.m. seemed to stretch forever. But, at last, Sophie gave the warning. 'He's coming!' she yelped. 'He's actually coming!' My kids and I were jumping with excitement. The doorbell rang and I signalled for calm. I smoothed myself and opened the door. 'Hiya neighbour,' I beamed in a slightly over the top Ned Flanders way. 'Happy Christmas Dave.'

He stepped through the door. 'Doesn't Christmas drag,' he said. 'And what nightmare weather?' Dave and family wiped their feet and came through into the kitchen. My kids were primed. Ollie went about getting drinks for the kids while Sophie took charge of Dave. 'We've got a new chair for Christmas,' she explained, leading him through to the conservatory. 'And, as guest of honour, you have to sit in it.'

Sophie led Dave to the positive chair. A strange anticipatory air filled the room. I glanced at my kids, their eyes shining, mouths agog. Dave's negative bottom was about to hit our positive chair. This might cause some sort of rift in the space–time continuum. Finally, he sat, his bum finding its home in our positive chair. And the world didn't end. A huge smile spread across Dave's face and we had a terrific hour of rollickingly happy chat. The first positive chat in eight years of next-door neighbourhoodism.

So, our final message is the chair knows. And so do you.

You know that, at your best, you are an inspiration to your family and friends. You light up your classroom and elevate learning to unprecedented levels.

You know that the challenges of primary teaching are huge but the rewards are even greater.

You know there is effort involved in being your best self. But now, more than ever, you know that effort is worth making.

ABOUT THE AUTHORS

Stuart Spendlow says that he absolutely loves his job because it's just so unique – every single teacher who supposedly 'does the same job' actually experiences an entirely different job. He absolutely loves his colleagues too – who have helped shape him into the teacher that he is. So far, he has worked as a literacy leader, computing coordinator and e-safety leader, and has appeared as a guest writer for various educational websites and publications, including *Teach Primary* magazine, *The Guardian*, the Literacy Shed blog, TTS Group and more.

Whenever he has some spare time, Stuart also works as a producer for his local theatre and enjoys playing the piano and drums (he can't read a single note of music but he's determined to be able to do it one day). Stuart also gets his hair cut every two weeks at the same place (in case that crops up in a random pub quiz somewhere), he has a small scar on his chin where no facial hair grows after cutting it open by falling into a supermarket freezer at the age of 6, and he can escape from a straitjacket in under forty-five seconds. Don't ask …

As well as teaching, Stuart has also found himself writing for children. His first children's book, *PENGUINPIG*, received acclaim from many, including BBC's *The Apprentice* star, Claude Littner, as being 'a must for schools, libraries and families with children'. In February 2015, it officially became an Amazon number one bestseller as schools rushed out to buy it to support their teaching of e-safety to young children.

Andy describes himself as a qualified teacher, accidental author, happiness expert and learning junkie. His 'Spy Dog' series has sold a million copies across the world and he has also penned a number of self-help books for adults and teenagers. Andy has been studying the science of positive psychology, culminating in a PhD at Loughborough University. His findings have fed into a series of workshops and keynotes, centring on the theme of 'The Art of Being Brilliant'.

Andy has two children and he is an avid supporter of Derby County Football Club. He is happy, but sometimes wonders how much happier he might have been if he'd supported a better team.

Andy's work is showcased at www.artofbrilliance.co.uk and you can follow his happiness tweets at @beingbrilliant.